THE EAGLE

Vicki Gibson

authorHOUSE®

AuthorHouse™ UK Ltd.
1663 Liberty Drive
Bloomington, IN 47403 USA
www.authorhouse.co.uk
Phone: 0800.197.4150

Published by AuthorHouse 09/24/2014

ISBN: 978-1-4969-9066-2 (sc)
ISBN: 978-1-4969-9067-9 (e)

THE HOLY BIBLE, NEW INTERNATIONAL VERSION®, NIV® Copyright © 1973, 1978, 1984, 2011 by Biblica, Inc.® Used by permission. All rights reserved worldwide.

CONTENTS

Chapter 1: The Taylor Family.. 1

Chapter 2: Jacob at School 6

Chapter 3: Rebekkah at School 10

Chapter 4: The Journey Home 17

Chapter 5: The Christening.. 22

Chapter 6: The Flight.. 30

Chapter 7: Jacob and the Nest... 36

Chapter 8: Rebekkah and the Nest 40

Chapter 9: The Tree 43

Chapter 10: Monday Morning - Rebekkah 51

Chapter 11: Monday Morning - Jacob.............................. 58

Chapter 12: Rebekkah's New School................................. 64

Chapter 13: Jacob's New School....................................... 71

Chapter 14: Rebekkah and Kirsty 75

Chapter 15: Jacob at the Factory.......................................81

Chapter 16: Jacob Returns to School................................ 94

Chapter 17: Jacob 100

Chapter 18: Jacob and Robert Seagull 108

Chapter 19: Rebekkah and Jacob 113

My thanks to my family for reading and reviewing this book and encouraging me to go forward with its publication. Also The Abbey Junior School and Bourne Academy for their insightful comments. And finally, Allan who proof read the whole thing.

Isaiah 40:31

But those who hope in the LORD will renew their strength. They will soar on **wings** like **eagles**; they will run and not grow weary, they will walk and not be faint.

CHAPTER 1

THE TAYLOR FAMILY

Rebekkah had had that dream again. In it she was flying high above the human world on the back of a majestic golden eagle. The fields below her stretched out like a huge patchwork quilt. Rivers meandered like huge snakes with neither head nor tail. The comparison made her shiver although she was not afraid. When she awoke she was troubled. Usually when she had the dream they were alone. This time she had had a sense of being followed by another bird. She had craned her neck from side to side moving as far as she dared whilst holding on to the feathers at the back of the eagle's neck. She had been unable to see anything. The dream ended abruptly when her brother crashed into the room.

'Bekkah, have you seen my shoes?' he stood at her door scowling. Jacob and Rebekkah Taylor lived at number 1 Madison Gardens. Neither liked the other. Given the choice, Jacob would have preferred a rat to his sister and Rebekkah would have liked a sister or a rabbit. Jacob was 12, red haired and a smaller version of his father. Rebekkah was ten, petite with a small button nose and long hair tied into a ponytail.

'No, I haven't and get out of my room.' She sat up in her bed, deftly wound her ponytail around her hand and retied it with a rubber band. Jacob strode into her space, banging the bedroom door against the wall as he entered. He attempted to open the door to the wardrobe. Rebekkah leapt out of bed and pushed her hand against the door. Enraged, he pushed her causing her to bang her head. She lashed out at him. Her mouth opened in a wide slash of lips and teeth. She screamed, knowing that at least one of her parents or maybe both would come to the rescue. Ignoring her, Jacob wrenched open the wardrobe door and began throwing things into the room.

'Jacob!' his father's voice boomed from the doorway. 'Stop that right now.'

Jacob responded by throwing even more items onto the floor. He figured he was already in trouble so he might as well make the most of it.

Rebekkah stood up, put her hands on her hips and screamed, 'Look what he's doing? Tell him! Tell him to put all that back!'

The older version of Jacob gritted his teeth and grabbed at his son, spinning him around so he could glare at him. 'Stop that now, you foul child. Go and get ready for school. I haven't got time for this. I have to go to work.' Mr Taylor's voice was loud and slightly squeaky. As usual he was more concerned about himself than his children. As Jacob slouched out of the room he turned slightly and smirked at his sister who howled at him. 'I hate you!' His father cuffed him round the ears as he walked past. 'Go and clean your teeth you horrible boy! Rebekkah, stop making that awful noise and get ready for school. We will be leaving in five minutes.'

They lived in a large, detached house with a small garden that they were only allowed to play in once they had finished their homework, read a chapter of a novel, done their music practice and tidied their rooms. Mr and Mrs Taylor were ambitious workaholics who probably should never have had children. They spent most of their time arguing about who was going to pick them up and whose turn it was to run them to whatever activity they were signed up to on any particular evening. Almost all the conversations were about what other people's children had achieved and how hard they were working to ensure Jacob and Rebekkah had a good future. Conversely Jacob and Rebekkah would talk about all the gadgets their friends had and demand to be taken to the latest film. This was not a happy family.

Jacob wandered into the bathroom. He had no intention of cleaning his teeth. He squeezed some toothpaste out and sucked it before spitting randomly into the sink. Some of it hit the wall and slid down towards the taps. Fascinated, he watched it. Then, sucking more from the tube, spat again, this time quite deliberately and watched to see how long the second would take to catch up with the first spit.

'You can clean that lot off right now!' Jacob jumped. His father had crept up on him unexpectedly. 'Go on, do it, you disgusting child!'

Jacob looked at his father. He saw a mirror image of himself only older. His dad had weird ears and a monobrow. If only his genes could have skipped the top part of his dad's head his life would have been so much better.

Reluctantly he cupped his hand under the tap and sloshed water over the wall. It ran down the tiles and into the sink taking some of the spit and toothpaste with it. His father reached past him, grabbed the toothbrush and scrubbed the wall with it. He then gave it back to his son.

'Aw dad, I can't use that brush now it's dirty!'

'Well you should have thought about that before you started playing dirty games. Do it...and hurry up. I have to go to work.'

Jacob looked at his father and then looked at the brush. He slowly and deliberately squeezed more toothpaste onto its head and raised it to his mouth. He calculated that his dad's need to humiliate him would be replaced by his need to get to work. He was right; his father turned on his heels and walked out. Jacob threw down the brush and, grinning at his small victory wandered off into his bedroom, where he flopped down onto his bed and began playing with his iPad, oblivious to the passage of time and his own need to catch a bus.

'Jacob! Jacob...are you ready? It's time to go. Hurry up! Put that thing away, get your shoes on, find your coat, get your bag.' His mother appeared at the door. Jacob ignored her. Now this was rude and ill-advised because his mother had a fiery temper and was quite capable of grounding him or worse. Right on cue she strode towards him, grabbed the offending article and slapped him round the head.

'Aw mum, that's the second time today I've been abused, you and dad are violent!' he whined.

'Do as you are told or, you won't get this back...ever.' She turned on her heels and stalked out of the room yelling at Rebekkah to hurry up.

Grumbling he got up and jammed his feet into his shoes without loosening the laces. This involved him in a lot of wriggling of his toes and sideways movement of the feet. His right foot went in quite easily but the left foot stubbornly refused to slot in. He hopped towards the door and then shuffled down the stairs, bag in hand. His mother was standing by the open door like a human coat hanger with his coat in her hand. She threw it at him and slammed the door inches from his foot and marched towards the car. His sister was already in the back seat.

Great, another day in paradise.

CHAPTER 2

JACOB AT SCHOOL

Jacob was bored by school. Most of what he was taught he thought pointless. The only subjects he valued were those involving science and maths. He could see a use for them. Why didn't they teach computer programming and engineering instead of history, english and religious education? RE was particularly pointless he thought to himself as he sat waiting for the teacher to arrive. Religion was for primitive people who had a need to explain the unexplainable. Now that we have science there is no need for such superstitious belief. And why inflict those beliefs on him? As if he wanted to know about how Muslims pray. Or, how to label the inside of a church? Nobody went to church now anyway. And Hinduism, what was that about? Their heroes seemed to be skinny men sitting around meditating, just so they could be reborn as something better. They needed to join the real world. This life is all there is. Religious people just needed to get over it.

He leant over to his friend and suggested they play a game on their phones while the lesson was on. The teacher bustled in. She was the Deputy Head but also taught RE. She wore tweed suits and a blouse that was too tight. Too much cake! Wouldn't it be funny if her buttons popped off? Jacob shared this thought with his friend who sniggered. Miss Preston was always disorganised and late. She claimed she had been seeing a parent but Jacob reckoned she had been in the staff room having another cup of tea and a biscuit. Her breath always smelled of tea.

'So, today we are going to talk about miracles. Can anyone tell me what a miracle is?'

Gertrude's hand shot straight up. Gertrude's family went to church. She was annoying. Jacob decided to interrupt before Gertrude answered the question.

'If my mum lets me have a lie-in on a Saturday.' He shouted. There was laughter, he sat forward pleased with the attention.

'Jacob, don't shout out! Put your hand up. Gertrude you were first.'

As expected, Gertrude had the right answer. 'It's when something happens against the laws of nature, Miss Preston. Like when Jesus healed the man with the withered arm.'

'Yes, that's right. Well done. Now we are going to read about some miracles and I want you to create a newspaper article of the event, writing about it as if you were there.'

Jacob groaned inwardly. This was just the sort of task he hated. He had to do something quickly to distract her and get some fun out of the lesson.

'Miss Preston, as there is no proof that miracles actually do happen can I write the article in such as way as to describe Jesus as a con man who tricks people?'

'No, you cannot Jacob. The point of the exercise is to describe accurately what you have seen and to use your imagination. Think how the people might have felt. They were poor, they had no doctors, and a man with a withered arm would not be able to work. This was a great act of kindness and would have changed his life and circumstances for ever.'

'Well that's the point Miss Preston; I haven't seen it have I and until I do I cannot believe that these things really happen. It's not like writing about David over there picking his nose. I can see that with my own eyes.' The class tittered and some laughed. Jacob sat back in his seat and picked up his pen. He began tapping it on the desk. He did this when agitated as it helped calm him down.

'Look David, I mean Jacob…this is not a philosophy lesson, if I wanted to discuss whether miracles happen then I would set you a different task. You need to be able to describe a miracle.'

'But Miss I can't describe something that I haven't seen or don't agree happened. Do you have any proof that miracles still happen today?'

Miss Preston was becoming increasingly flustered and two little pink marks appeared on her cheeks just underneath her eyes. 'Well, there's the miracle of creation and the wonderful miracle of birth.'

'But Miss, didn't you just say that a miracle is against the laws of nature...there's a perfectly natural explanation for birth.' He paused for effect, looking around the class with a knowing grin. 'And the earth was caused by the Big Bang not God.'

The class were listening attentively, enjoying the entertainment. Gertrude came to her beleaguered teacher's defence. 'There is a man in our church who was healed of cancer after we prayed for him. The doctors said it was a miracle because he only had a few days to live and they had given up on him.'

'Yes! Good! That's a wonderful example Gertrude, thank you. Now class, let's get on with the task we only have a few minutes left. That includes you Jacob. I shall be reading yours first.'

Jacob opened his mouth and then shut it.

He would get Gertrude later.

CHAPTER 3

REBEKKAH AT SCHOOL

Rebekkah loved school. She had a little crush on her teacher who was calm, kind and enthusiastic. Whatever Rebekkah did she seemed delighted with. This was in stark contrast to her mother who was always critical and was hard to please. Rebekkah ran into school and found her peg. There was the usual chatter and excitement interspersed by squeals of delight when someone showed something especially cute on their phone.

'Look Bekkah, Grace has a Labrador puppy, isn't she adorable?' Rebekkah hung up her coat and dropped her bag on the floor. She adjusted her ponytail and then peered at the tiny image on the screen as it was thrust into her face. 'Mmm…oh she's so beautiful. What's her name?'

'Honey.'

'Awww that's so cute.' The bell went for morning school, Rebekkah slipped her arm into her friend's and they ran towards the classroom door expecting to see Miss Bates who usually stood in the entrance to greet them. Instead there was a different teacher who they had never seen before.

'Hello girls I am your teacher today. Miss Bates is unwell.' Rebekkah's heart sank. Her feelings about the day ahead immediately took a nosedive. The teacher turned to Rebekkah and Grace.

'That's not really an appropriate way to come into the classroom is it? We are not babies. Go back into the cloakroom and come in properly as befits girls of your age.'

Grace and Rebekkah unlinked arms and slowly went back into the cloakroom. They looked at each other and Rebekkah pulled a face.

'She's a bit of a witch isn't she? Miss Bates never minds us linking arms. Who does she think she is? Old bat, she looks about 90 and did you see that wart on the end of her nose? Wouldn't want to get too close to her on a dark night...' Rebekkah tailed off as she noticed the look of horror on her friend's face. Slowly she turned round to find the battleaxe standing right behind her. She had a weird look on her face.

'Get in the classroom both of you; we haven't got all day. Your parents are not paying for you to stand here gossiping. I thought you would have better manners than this. I shall be keeping my eye on you two and don't think you are sitting together; collect your things and sit away from each other.'

Rebekkah felt tears prickling at the back of her eyes.

'But Miss…' she realised she had no idea what the teacher was called. 'Miss Bates always lets us sit together.'

'Miss. Bates is not here and she is clearly far too soft with you. Hurry up or you will be sitting in the corridor. And my name is Miss Cannon.'

The lesson did not improve. It was clear Miss Cannon had no intention of forgetting and forgiving. She took every opportunity to pick holes in Rebekkah's work. In English she stood at Rebekkah's shoulder reading every word. Every so often she would point out an error in punctuation or tut loudly when she spelt something wrong. At one stage she threw a dictionary at her. In maths she asked Rebekkah to answer the most difficult questions and when she stammered that she did not understand, rolled her eyes upwards questioning whether she had been awake in any of her lessons. By lunchtime Rebekkah was a nervous wreck. She and Grace went off to the nurse together but to their horror found Miss Cannon sitting with Mrs Band chatting, laughing and drinking a cup of tea together. The nurse looked up at the two girls as they came in. Grace looked at Rebekkah and rather lamely said, 'Rebekkah has a tummy ache.'

Miss Cannon fixed her small piggy eyes on Rebekkah. 'These two are hypochondriacs, Stephanie. I have been teaching them all morning and neither of them complained of anything wrong. I think they are just trying to get out of their afternoon lessons. Don't worry; I shall make sure they have plenty to do to keep their mind off themselves. Don't be so weak girls.'

The nurse looked at Miss Cannon and then back to Rebekkah. Impatiently she waved them both away. To her horror Rebekkah realised she was also scared of Miss Cannon and there would be no refuge in her office.

The afternoon was no better. In science she was forced to work with Freda. How did Miss Cannon know that no one wanted to work with Freda? Freda was a loner and preferred to work on her own. She tried to control everything and would not share. She also went into long complicated explanations about things that were completely irrelevant and used long words that Rebekkah did not understand. Once Miss Bates had gathered the class together and had tried to explain that Freda was a bit different to other children. She found it difficult to make friends and they should all make a special effort with her. Rebekkah made a special effort to avoid her.

They were studying the body's circulation system. They had to find each other's pulses and explain why, after exercise, the pulse rate got quicker. As evidence, they had to take each other's pulses and write down the resting rate and then the new rate after exercising. With Grace this would have been fun but Freda hated anyone touching her and insisted on taking her own pulse rate. First of all, she could not find it and pulled back sharply from Rebekkah when she tried to help. When she did find the little beat in her wrist she went white as a sheet and had to sit down.

'What's the matter now?' Rebekkah was getting really frustrated and worried that Miss Cannon would tell them off if they did not complete the task.

'I don't like the feeling of it.'

Frustrated, Rebekkah grabbed her wrist. 'Come on; don't be so silly. You can't see the blood. It's underneath your skin.'

Freda snatched her hand away from Rebekkah and started screaming. 'I told you not to touch me. I told you not to touch me. No one understands.'

Then the dreaded thing happened. Miss Cannon strode over to them both. Legs astride, hands on hips, piggy eyes glaring, she descended on Rebekkah.

'What have you done to Freda, you wicked girl?' Freda was now building up to a crescendo.

Miss Cannon moved towards her. Scared that she might be touched again, Freda ran out of the classroom and down the corridor wailing.

'This is all your fault,' hissed Miss Cannon. Pointing at Grace she ordered her to go and get the nurse while telling Rebekkah to sit down. 'I'll deal with you later.'

Rebekkah really did feel sick now. The class were completely silent and stared at her. It seemed an eternity before the nurse arrived, red in the face and out of breath. Rebekkah wondered what her pulse rate would be at this moment in time.

Miss Cannon stepped outside the classroom so no one could hear the conversation. Meanwhile from the classroom window Freda could be seen running down the road towards the bus stop. A few moments later the nurse could be seen running down the road after her. It would have been funny had Rebekkah not been so scared. Miss Cannon came back in and closed the door.

'That's it girls, the show is over.'

'But Miss, will Freda be alright?' asked Claire.

'Of course she will be. The nurse is with her. That's no thanks to you though, Rebekkah. The bell is about to go. Pack up everyone but not you Rebekkah. I am not done with you yet.'

Everyone rushed out. Rebekkah slowly packed her things away into her bag. Her hands were shaking; she wished she were on the bus and a zillion miles from school.

Miss Cannon wandered around the room tapping her stubby fingers on the tabletops. She was humming to herself. It suddenly dawned on Rebekkah that she was stretching the moment to create maximum tension. Torn between fear and anxiety about missing her bus she eventually plucked up the courage to speak.

'Miss Cannon, I have a bus to catch and my brother will be waiting for me.' She looked up at the woman standing just two desks away from her. She had a strange smile on her face, almost menacing.

'Rebekkah, today has not been a good day. You have got off to a very bad start with me. Miss Bates will be away for some time and I shall be your teacher. I don't like what I see of you but you must have some redeeming features. So far, you appear to me to be dim, rude and impossible to work with. I don't think you should be here. You need to show me that you deserve your place at this highly academic and well thought of school. We don't want numbskulls like you bringing down its reputation. Over the weekend you will do some research on the circulation of blood in the human body. I expect a three hundred-word essay on it. No cut and paste from the Internet. It will be your own words. Do you understand?'

Rebekkah nodded glumly, picked up her school bag and ran out the door. She caught the bus by the skin of her teeth.

Chapter 4

The Journey Home

On leaving school Jacob stopped by the school garden to collect a few unmentionables. He still had revenge in mind for Gertrude and her friends. The bus arrived and he noted with glee that the driver was Old Spike. He was only interested in getting them home as fast as possible. He would stop for nothing.

The bus journey proved to be hugely entertaining. Jacob had somehow got hold of some worms and spent the journey dropping them onto various unsuspecting girls. Soon, the bus was in uproar with children squealing and shrieking. The bus driver had tried yelling for everyone to sit down and be quiet but this only added to the pandemonium. In the end, much against his natural instinct to just drive on regardless, he was forced to pull over and find out what all the fuss was about. He was a tall thin man with heavily greased spiky hair that stood on end. His face was already red and sweaty from the exertion of shouting. He marched down the aisle of the bus halting only to pick up a few of the wriggling creatures that he ejected through an open window. It did not take long for him to find out that Jacob was the culprit. He had ill advisedly (as Jacob knew his rights) grabbed the boy by his arm and dragged him down to the front of the bus where he shoved him onto an empty seat. Muttering about rude, middle class twerps with too much money, the driver had demanded to know his full name.

When Jacob got home his mother was standing at the door waiting for him. She did not look at all happy. Apparently the bus driver had phoned school and they in turn had then phoned home. Jacob was sent to bed without any tea. When Jacob protested that the bus driver had manhandled him and called him a middle class twerp his father cuffed him across the ear and said that he was a spoilt brat. He then got a lecture about how lucky he was because when his father was a lad they used to cane boys like him. Anyway, time out in his room wasn't so bad as he had stashed away a box of sweets and biscuits for just such an occasion as this and it was better than lamb stew any day! It also got him out of the agony of dinnertime conversation and nags about manners.

Rebekkah, left on her own with her parents found dinnertime interminable. They were arguing and bickering about plans for the weekend. Apparently, they had all been invited to a christening. Her father did not want to go because he said it would be boring and he had loads of work to do. Her mother had snapped back at him that she had had to sit through his mother's 80th birthday with all his dreadful relatives and at least this was a celebration of the beginning of life not the end when she was going senile. Rebekkah was quite interested in the event itself.

'What's a christening?' she had asked. She was quite horrified by the answer - a child, against her will, was splashed with cold water and oil but apparently (according to dad) this was preferable to circumcision which Jews and Muslims did to induct their children into the faith. Part of her wished it was a circumcision as it would have been fun to see Jacob's reaction. She carried her plate to the sink and excused herself as she had a lot of homework to do. That always worked.

Saturday passed uneventfully. Jacob was grounded and spent the day in his room. Rebekkah did her homework and then sat watching TV. She liked Saturdays as she could catch up on all the programmes missed during the week.

That night she slept fitfully and dreamt extensively. She was constantly being chased, by whom she had no idea, but there was an ominous presence, a darkness from which she could not escape. She would run but seemed to make no progress. The darkness just got closer. Afraid, she called out for help. Then, as if from nowhere, a huge bird descended from the sky and caught her in its talons. Moving soundlessly through the air she was aware of being tightly held and very safe. After a while a tree came into view and the bird dropped her into it. The branches shook and snapped as she bounced from one to another.

Then a voice broke into her dream. 'Rebekkah, Rebekkah. Wake up. We need to get going.' She opened her eyes to see her mother's face looming over her. The shaking was caused by her mother who had her by the shoulder and was roughly pushing at her. Rebekkah groaned and turned over. At least it was not Monday.

Over breakfast she tried to talk to Jacob. He was grumpy and uncommunicative.

'Jacob, have you ever had a dream that you can remember?'

He reached in front of her and grabbed some toast. He slapped some butter on it and then stuck the buttery knife in the honey leaving yellow streaks in its golden syrup. Normally she would have told on him, mother would be cross that he had not used the honey spoon. However today she swallowed her indignation and tried again.

'Jacob? Have you ever had a dream that you can remember?'

'No.' He said shortly munching his way through the toast. She watched as the over laden bread released a trickle of honey down the side of his hand.

'Jacob, lick your hand before it goes on the cloth.' For once he did as he was told. She pressed on, hoping his compliance might mean a conversation. 'Last night I dreamt that a large bird saved me.'

'Saved you? From what?' Jacob mumbled as he licked the honey off his hand.

'Well, that's just it. I don't really know. I was being chased by something. Something dark and horrible and the bird scooped me up in her claws and saved me. It was so real.'

'Jacob stared at her.' He lowered his voice to a whisper and leaned in close. 'Something dark and horrible,' he whispered.

And then he paused for effect. 'Do you mean...LIKE THIS!' He roared; twisting his face into a grotesque shape, tongue out, teeth bared. Rebekkah screamed.

Mother looked up from her paper and yelled at them both to go and get ready for church.

Chapter 5

The Christening

It was a beautiful warm and sunny day. Everyone looked smart if a little grumpy as they drove to the church. Jacob was ominously quiet; probably planning something, thought Rebekkah. She was upset that he had not taken her dream seriously; she had also been told about the worm incident and was not at all surprised as Jacob frequently played tricks on her. It served him right and she hoped he would get punished at school as well.

The church was old with beautiful stone arches. The inside smelt musty and was cool after the warmth outside. Rebekkah waited for her eyes to adjust to the light. It was very beautiful with sweeping arches made of a rich, dark wood. Her eyes were drawn upwards to the ceiling that was extremely high and shaped like an upturned boat. The family were welcomed by a smiley lady who gave them a sheet of paper and a book. Her mother was busy scanning the congregation, looking for a familiar face while her father stood and scowled. His mood was as dark as the wooden pews they were ushered towards. Jacob picked up the cushion that was at everyone's feet and sat on it. Mother jabbed him in the ribs and bringing her face very close to his so others could not hear, hissed at him to put it back. Apparently it was for kneeling on not sitting. Rebekkah thought that on this occasion Jacob was right. She would have had a better view if she had been elevated on the cushion. She sighed audibly when a very tall man and his family sat in front of her.

'Great,' said Jacob, 'can't see anything, can't speak, can't play games; welcome to the house of fun.'

The man must have heard because he shifted sideways so that he was sitting in front of father.

'Oh well,' thought Rebekkah. 'That's better, and dad doesn't want to be here anyway.

The service was a sandwich of hymns, prayers and readings. The vicar, a jolly man dressed in a white dress with a collar was doing his utmost to be entertaining. But he was not. Instead, Rebekkah found herself fascinated by the lectern from which the Bible was read. It was made out of brass and perched on top of it was a magnificent eagle standing with its wings spread out and its neck raised. It looked up into the ceiling as if it longed to be free of the burden on its back. As she stared at it she realised that it was very similar to the bird in her dream. Then an odd thing happened. She could have sworn that it winked at her. She studied it intently and then, it happened again; the silver bird winked at her. Closing her eyes she found herself imagining what it would be like to fly with the eagle. The church slipped away with its musty smell and hushed voices. Instead she could feel the air rushing into her face, the rhythm of its wings, while beneath her the earth rushed by.

'Oh eagle,' she murmured. 'Take me away from school so I don't have to see Miss Cannon again.'

Jacob poked her in the ribs. 'Look! This is more like it!'

Rebekkah jumped. Snatched rudely from her dream, she glowered at Jacob but her attention was immediately grabbed by the spectacle of the child who was soon to be christened running gleefully along the front of the church. His mother, uncertain what to do and not wanting to draw attention to herself, bent low as if avoiding divine fire and ran after him. He, thinking it a game ran even faster and began to chuckle. Rebekkah looked at the vicar who carried on talking while his eyes followed the little child. All eyes were now on the chase. The toddler, finding his way barred by adults, dropped to his knees and scampered up the stairs past the wrought iron rail where worshippers had knelt before their God for centuries and up to the altar. He scampered under the white tablecloth, which swallowed him up. His mother, now a deep shade of pink dropped to her knees and peeped under the table. He shuffled backwards on his bottom so as to avoid her grasp.

'The only way she is going to get that kid is if she goes under the table herself,' whispered Jacob. He was sitting forward in his seat, eyes glittering with enjoyment.

Sure enough, the woman, after several wild sweeps of the hand under the cloth, ducked her head and crawled under the table. There was a scream of rage; the cloth bulged to the left and then, out they both came, like Jonah from the mouth of the whale. She was red in the face and he was absolutely furious at losing the game. The vicar, undeterred, cleared his throat and bellowed above the noise.

'Now, as we move into the next bit of our service there's something I would like to show you all.' Seemingly oblivious to the uproar around him, he scooped his hand under his cassock and triumphantly, as if he were God himself and had just created it from nothing, held up a small bottle.

'This, he said, is holy water, brought from the River Jordan itself.' He paused dramatically for effect. One or two adults looked up but most continued to watch the pantomime of mother with child who had now reached the pew from which the escape had been made.

Pressing on the vicar asked, 'Now children, who can tell me what is special about the River Jordan?' Silence, only broken by the hiccoughing of the star of the show, who had been given some chocolate to eat as a distraction.

His father leaned towards Jacob. 'It's where Jesus was baptised,' Jacob glowered at his father. 'I'm not saying that, I'll look like I'm a member of the God Squad. You say it.'

Rebekkah had her hand up. 'It's where Jesus was baptised in Israel.' The vicar beamed at her. Her father looked at her and winked. Jacob raised his eyes upwards in disgust. Mother smiled indulgently at her daughter. The private education was paying off. She looked around to ensure that everyone had noticed that it was her daughter who had answered the question.

The vicar raised his arms and swept to the back of the church. 'Follow me,' he called, 'we are now going to baptise young David using drops of water that have come from the very same river in which our Lord Jesus was baptised. Children, come to the front so you can see what's happening. Adults, please make room for the children.'

Rebekkah shyly joined the children while Jacob hung back. The vicar stood behind the font, which looked to Jacob like a large birdbath. The parents of little David joined him. David's dad was holding him tightly lest he run off again. The child had a chocolate dribble emerging from his mouth. Jacob watched; fascinated by the gooey mess that dripped into the waters of the font. An older lady in a white smock reached forward with a tissue and tapped the mother on the arm. Confused, the mother looked at the lady who nodded encouragingly towards the child's mouth while touching her own lips.

Little David, however, was distracted by a large swinging chain at the bottom of which was a bauble containing incense. It was perilously close to his fingers and Jacob willed him to grab it and swing from it. The boy, distracted by the large ornate silvery bowl was taken unawares when the vicar began daubing his forehead with oil and then splashed some water over his head. The little boy's lips puckered and he reached over to his mother calling for her. The vicar quickly lit a candle and gave it to the dad to hold while mum turned sideways to allow David a better view of the light. The toddler, once again made bold by distraction, reached over to grab the candle that dropped from its holder and with a loud plop fell into the font. There was an audible gasp from the watching congregation. Jacob grinned. The vicar, ever the true professional, pressed on regardless. A steamroller came to mind.

Finally, it was over and they could eat.

Jacob and Rebekkah sat in a corner as near to the food as they could get without being conspicuous. They did not talk; they had nothing to say to each other. Rebekkah got up to help herself to more food and as she rejoined her brother at the table he groaned.

'Look out, that vicar's coming this way.' Sure enough he stopped at their table.

'Enjoying the chocolate cake?' He enquired.

Jacob took a huge bite and nodded hoping this would deter the man from asking him any more questions.

Instead he pulled up a chair and turned to Rebekkah. 'You're the girl who answered my question about the River Jordan aren't you?'

Rebekkah nodded.

'Have you ever been to the Holy Land?'

Jacob could not resist having a pop at this man who held such ridiculous beliefs. His mouth, now empty, blurted out: 'The Holy Land. Why is it called that? No land is holy. All land is the same.'

The vicar looked at him. 'Well, it's where our Lord was born and so that makes it unique and special to God.'

'I don't believe there is a God and if there's no God then it's not holy is it?'

Rebekkah squirmed, 'Jacob that's not very polite.'

'No, that's all right. I can understand why you might think that. What's your name?'

'Jacob'.

'Jacob, why don't you believe there is a God?'

'Because I can't believe in something I can't see.'

'When we look at a beautiful painting, we don't have to know or see the artist to know someone painted it. Isn't it the same with earth? It is a beautiful and well-designed place. Surely a being with creativity and imagination must have created it?'

'Why? Science tells us that it evolved. Anyway the earth isn't well designed. There are earthquakes and volcanoes. Would you excuse me for a minute I need to go to the bathroom?'

Jacob stood up and went to the toilet. On his return he found the vicar in earnest conversation with his sister. He tripped as he approached the table and put his hand out to save himself from falling to the floor. In so doing his hand pressed against the vicar's back.

'Are you okay Jacob? Good job I was here or you could have had a nasty fall. Anyway nice talking to you both, enjoy the rest of your day.' The man stood up and as he turned away Rebekkah could see that a piece of paper appeared to be stuck to his jumper.

On it were written the words: *I think stupid things therefore I am stupid.*

'Oh Jacob that's so rude', gasped Rebekkah.

'He's an idiot,' sneered Jacob. 'Don't tell me you believe in all those fairy stories too?'

'No! Of course not,' she stammered, 'But my teacher Miss Bates says that she has seen an angel and she talks to God.'

Jacob mimicked her: 'my teacher says...Miss Bates says... but you haven't, have you? She's just as barmy as that vicar and so are you. It's because you are a girl, girls are soft in the head.'

'Jacob!' His father's voice interrupted him; 'I want a word with you.'

CHAPTER 6

THE FLIGHT

Jacob was sent to bed as soon as they got home. Apparently he was a disgrace and an embarrassment. His sister on the other hand was the best daughter any parent could wish to have. 'Little do they know,' thought Jacob; 'She makes things up and lies.'

He reached under the pillow for the small electronic gadget he had hidden and switched it on.

He could hear his parents talking loudly downstairs. If Jacob had been more sensitive he would have listened in and heard them arguing. However the adult world was of no interest to him. He was briefly aware of a plate being dropped on the floor and a shout, which he assumed, was of annoyance at the breakage. There were some clanking noises as mum emptied the dishwasher and then, silence. He guessed they were both working...at least they would not be back upstairs and bothering him.

Absorbed in his game he was unaware of the strange glow that appeared outside his window and was startled by a gentle tapping against the frame. Curious, he swung his legs out of the bed and peeked underneath the curtain. Two unblinking orange eyes looked back at him. Startled, he dropped the curtain and drew back into bed. His first inclination was to shout but something held him back and he did not. Dad was in no mood for jokes and if he called out and it turned out that nothing was there, he would be grounded for a zillion years. No, he would have to look again. Slowly he pulled back the curtain and then he saw it; a beautiful golden eagle was peering through the glass at him.

'God! You scared me', he said and then to his surprise the bird answered him. 'Don't be afraid, Jacob'.

'You spoke! You can speak! I must be dreaming. I can't believe this is happening to me.'

'Jacob? Jacob? Who are you talking to?' It was Rebekkah. Excited, Jacob jumped out of bed and ran to the door.

'Look out of the window, there's an eagle outside.' It was odd, when he later replayed it in his mind, that he never thought she might scream or scoff at him. They so rarely shared any moments of childhood intimacy or affection that he suddenly felt shy and a bit embarrassed.

Rebekkah, unaware of her brother's sudden discomfort, ran to the window and looked out.

'Oh,' she gasped and took a step back in shock. 'There is a huge bird outside; it's trying to say something.'

'You can hear it too'? Jacob looked at her in shock. His little sister, usually so babyish and infantile suddenly seemed older and surprisingly unafraid. He was not sure what he expected when he invited her in to his room; screams perhaps but not this.

'This is the same eagle that I saw in my dream. You know, the one I told you about this morning, over breakfast. Oh Jacob this is amazing!'

Jacob opened his mouth to say something sarcastic and then promptly shut it. He turned back to the window and looked at the eagle waiting patiently for a response. Gingerly he flicked the catch on the casement and pushed it open. The eagle stepped to one side, her claws balancing on the window ledge.

'Hello Rebekkah, we meet again. Are you ready to fly?'

'Oh yes, please,' said Rebekkah instinctively. 'Can I climb on your back? Come on, Jacob!'

'Wait a minute,' stammered Jacob.

'What is all this about?' He thought quickly. 'I must be dreaming. That's it. I fell asleep and now Rebekkah is in my dream. A bit weird especially after we had been talking about dreams.'

He pinched himself. Meanwhile Rebekkah had climbed onto the eagle's back and settled herself deep within the soft feathers.

'Oh come on, Jacob, it's like being in a gigantic feather bed.' Carefully he edged out of the window and placed a cautious foot on the eagle's back. The huge bird, as if waiting for this, reached behind her picked him up with her beak and placed him behind Rebekkah on her back. He then felt the tension in her muscles as she sprang off the windowsill and soared into the night sky. Terrified, he grabbed as many feathers as he could and crouched down into the downy forest of bony fluff. It was hard to keep still as the motion of the wings meant he could feel his seat moving up and down.

'Relax.' called the great bird. 'The more you fight the movement the more tired you will become. You won't fall. Let go and lie back. Copy your sister!'

Sure enough, Rebekkah seemed to have done this before, she was lying back and gazing up at the stars. 'Isn't it beautiful, Jacob?' she whispered.

'Where are we going? Where are you taking us?' Jacob shouted, unable to relax and still holding on for dear life.

The eagle turned its head slightly so Jacob could hear her above the rushing wind. 'To the nest.'

And that was it. Air rushed past Jacob's head. He was glad it was dark so he couldn't see the ground. He didn't have a great head for heights. His stomach was surging between

33

feelings of excitement and terror. At one point he thought he was actually going to be sick but fortunately this subsided. He was bemused as to how his baby sister could be so calm. He would have liked to talk to her but he was scared of moving in case he fell off and tumbled to the ground. He examined the eagle as she flew; her wings were enormous and well out of proportion to the rest of her. She had a short neck, which she kept steady while flying. He suddenly realised why the flight was so smooth; after the initial flapping to get them aloft she was actually gliding. She appeared to be using the minimum of effort to soar. He remembered reading somewhere that eagles used updrafts and thermals to move. Her centre of gravity was between the wings. His dad had told him that sitting over the wing on a plane was statistically the safest part of an aircraft. As his mind began to work once more, logic took over and he began to relax. They were lying between the wings; they were safe.

In what seemed like an age, they just lay and watched the stars. He had a sense of being very small in a wondrous universe. He had never felt like that before. A shooting star careered across the sky and headed into the enormous vastness of space. He wanted to cry with the sheer joy of it all. And then, as abruptly as it had started, the journey ended. The eagle suddenly adjusted her position and began to flap her wings; she appeared to be descending. After several moments of complete and utter terror she lowered her feet and swooped at speed into a tree and landed gracefully in a large nest. Rolling from side to side she shook her feathers vigorously and deposited them both on the floor. They appeared to have arrived.

'Now sleep,' she said. 'You must both be exhausted. There will be plenty of time for talking in the morning.' With that she gently picked up each child by their pyjama tops and placed them carefully onto a feather bed. Both children slept.

CHAPTER 7

JACOB AND THE NEST

Jacob was woken by a nudging movement. Slowly he opened his eyes and then shot bolt upright on his bed. A few feathers floated lazily up in the air and just as slowly descended back to earth. The eagle stared at him with her big orange eyes, only this time it was daylight and he could see her hooked beak and talons. He edged himself into a corner.

'Please don't hurt me,' he thought.

The eagle laughed, a rich sonorous sound that reverberated around the nest. 'Jacob, if I had wanted to hurt you I would have already done so. You are my friend and my guest. Your sister is already awake. Come, let us take a walk together.'

The eagle bounced from one foot to another, her claws spread like starfish on the uneven ground. Jacob stole a sideways look at her. He had never been so close to such a majestic bird of prey. Her head and neck pushed forward as she strutted along. Her legs were strong, the feathers hung like baggy trousers. Her wings were pressed against her sides.

Jacob thought she looked far less intimidating than she had done last night. Her head was large for a bird, her beak and eyes moved from side to side as she walked. He could see that she was taking everything in, clearly constantly assessing all about her. Jacob had to run to keep up.

The eagle told Jacob that as her guest he could go wherever he wanted and eat whatever he wanted. However there was one rule. In the centre of the garden grew a tree. This tree had the appearance of holding good fruit but eating from it would bring dire consequences. Jacob wanted to know why. His instinct was always to challenge any instruction that came without a clear and reasoned explanation. The eagle stopped and turned to face him. Breathing deeply he looked deep into her eyes. Her gaze was steady, unblinking and uncompromising. What he saw filled him with fear and he looked away.

After a long uncomfortable pause the eagle finally spoke.

'You will know the tree by its golden trunk and silver leaves. There are no others quite like it. Jacob, listen to me. Do not eat anything that you find growing on that tree however attractive or tasty it may appear. Do you understand? If you do then I can no longer protect you here.'

Then with a flap of her wings she was gone.

Jacob was troubled by the way the eagle had spoken to him. He was accustomed to being told off but this was different. It was as if the eagle had looked deep within him and found a dark shadow in his soul.

He shook himself. It was time to stop this ridiculous introspection. He did not believe in a soul anyway. He looked around him. There were trees to climb. His parents had always told him not to climb trees in case he fell or tore his trousers. But here he could do what he liked. Joyously he ran to a tree and grasped the gnarled trunk. His fingers found a crevice, he lifted his right foot onto a knobbly bit and up he went. Exhilarated he climbed and he climbed until he found himself swinging in the very tops of the trees. The view was fantastic, he could see for miles. To his right he caught sight of a river with a boat. Another thing his parents had told him he could not do was swim in a fresh water river in case he got a stomach upset or a chill. Excitedly he dropped from branch to branch and landed with a thump on the ground. He ran towards the river, untied the boat, grabbed the fishing net and pushed off. Under the seat was a hamper. Opening it he found all his favourite food inside; hot chip butties and ketchup, crisps, little sausages and jelly all to be washed down with real lemonade. He had a great feeling of liberation as he ate the food and tucked the hamper back under the seat. He peered over the side of the boat into the glistening water. Fish darted under the boat and out the other side as if to say, join us. He pulled off his clothes and jumped into the water gasping at the delicious coolness. This was fun!

He took a deep breath and dived to the bottom of the river touching the smooth stones with his hands. He was a good swimmer. He picked up a large flat one and burst up into the open water. Grabbing the boat he hauled himself in and flopped down inside. He examined the stone; it was beautiful and would make a good skimmer. He popped it into his pocket and dried it off in the warm sunshine. This place is like heaven he thought to himself. He picked up the net and poked it over the side of the boat. A fish swam into it and he lifted it out of the water. As he reached into the net he thought the fish spoke to him. 'Well done. But now put me back. Everything here must live.' He hesitated for a moment and then tipped the net upside down and watched the fish wriggle away. It seemed to pause and turn back to him before disappearing under a stone. He squeezed his eyes shut and tipped his head on one side to empty the water from his ear. This place is weird he thought to himself. Talking birds and fish. Weird.

CHAPTER 8

REBEKKAH AND THE NEST

Rebekkah had woken before her brother. Deciding not to wake him, she wandered outside. A beautiful scene greeted her. There was a meadow to her left with a carpet of pretty wild flowers and, to her right, was a wood. She could hear the trickling of a stream in the distance. To her delight, there were animals everywhere and none of them seemed afraid of her. There were lambs in the meadow darting in and out of the carpet of flowers shaded yellow and blue. She watched as they gambolled around their mothers nudging at their nipples and trying to access milk. She gasped as she noticed a lion in the distance. He looked at her and then opened his mouth and yawned. Lazily turning onto his back so his tummy faced the sun he stretched and rolled in the dust and then flicked himself over onto his haunches. 'Just like a huge pussy cat,' she thought to herself.

'Good morning Rebekkah, are you enjoying the nest?' She jumped at the unexpected interruption and turned to see the eagle standing nearby.

'Oh eagle,' she said, 'you made me jump. This place is amazing. Why doesn't the lion eat the lambs?'

The eagle laughed her rich, throaty laugh and with a jerk of her head indicated that Rebekkah should follow her. She ran to catch up and then the eagle paused to allow her to walk beside her.

'So, Rebekkah, you and I have met before.'

'We have?' she responded, puzzled. And then light dawned, 'Oh yes! You mean in church and in my dreams? But you weren't real then as you are now.'

'What's real Rebekkah?'

'Well, Jacob would say something is only real if you can touch it or see it with your own eyes.'

'Ah Jacob,' mused the eagle, 'and you, what do you say?'

'Well, unless I am dreaming this seems to be real. I can touch you, and see you. So, you are real. But…'

'Yes?'

'It's not normal. All this is not normal. The lion should be eating the lamb. The lamb should be afraid. You shouldn't be able to talk. We shouldn't be here. We should be at home in bed…'

'Ah,' said the eagle, 'and here's the thing. It's normal for you because you only see things from your world's point of view. Here in this world these things are normal. Come, let me show you around. Are you hungry?' The eagle hopped over to a table and tapped three times with her beak. In an instant the table was filled with all her favourite food. She gasped in astonishment as chocolate croissants, fresh and soft, burst out of nowhere. A jug of strawberry milk tipped itself into a glass. Toast and marmalade piled itself up onto a plate.

'Tuck in Rebekkah, and enjoy this place. You may go anywhere you like and eat anything you like. Except, in the centre of the nest there is a tree. You will know the tree by its golden trunk and silver branches. You must stay away from its fruit. It is the tree of knowledge of good and evil. If you eat of its fruit you will be unable to remain in the nest. Is that understood?'

Rebekkah nodded vigorously. Her one thought was that she could avoid going back to school and seeing that dreadful Miss Cannon again. 'I won't eagle. I promise I will be good.'

The eagle looked at her long and hard and then with a bounce and a flex of her long muscular legs shot up into the air and flew off. Rebekkah breathed deeply and smiled. She ate her fill of breakfast and then wandered into the woods.

She was in heaven.

CHAPTER 9

THE TREE

Meanwhile, Jacob was growing tired of the water. Picking up the oars he rowed to shore and jumped out. His thoughts turned to his sister who he had not seen that day. Not usually given to much affection for her he found himself wondering whether she was all right and headed off into the woods.

'Rebekkah!' he called. 'Rebekkah!'

'Over here,' came the reply.

He followed the sound and as he came into a clearing he saw her seated on a large trunk playing with squirrels and rabbits. 'Oh look Jacob. Aren't they cute? Come and play with us.' He approached her warily biting back the cutting remark that would normally flow from his lips about rabbit stew and cotton buds. He sat down next to her and watched her feed a carrot to one rather substantial rabbit.

'Bekks...' he said and paused. She looked at him in surprise, he never called her that. 'What do you think of this place? It's weird. It's like...' his words trailed off.

'Heaven,' she finished the sentence for him.

'Well, yes, except I don't believe in heaven,' he said, rather lamely.

'No?' She looked at him out of the corner of her eye. 'So how do these creatures talk? How did we get here? What is this place?'

The logical and rational side of his brain hunted for an answer. 'Maybe it's a dream that we are both sharing. You know, you exist in my dream.'

Rebekkah looked at him and sighed. 'Oh Jacob you are annoying, why can't you just believe?'

He changed the subject. 'Hey! Why don't we play hide and seek?'

'Ok, you go and hide and I'll count.'

Jacob ran off into the woods. He couldn't be sure but he thought he saw a flash of yellow in the undergrowth and then it was gone. Probably a snake he thought to himself and for some reason a shiver moved down his spine. What if there were snakes in this place? What if the eagle was lying and there were dangerous things in the woods. What if

there were poisonous snakes and dangerous creatures? Why
should he trust the eagle?

'Eight, nine, ten... coming, ready or not', his sister's voice
broke into his thoughts. A thought came to him. Would not
it be fun to hide and then scare her? Looking around him he
saw a golden tree in an open glade in front of him. He ran
towards it. He looked up at its delicate lung like branches.
They sparkled and shimmered in the sun like silver. And
then it came to him. This must be the tree that the eagle
had told him about. He hesitated but then curiosity got
the better of him. He approached it and laid his hands on
the golden trunk. It was smooth and shiny. Surprisingly he
felt no fear or anxiety. Surely, if this was such a dangerous
tree then he would feel something? He looked up into its
silvery branches and there high above his head he could see
an enormous pear. It appeared to be made of chocolate.
Certainly it was not a normal pear but then nothing was
normal here. He looked furtively over his shoulder and
could hear Rebekkah crashing about in the woods behind
him. The thought occurred to him that the eagle had said
nothing about climbing the tree only about the fruit itself.
No sooner had the thought entered his brain than his eyes
fell upon some golden whorls on the tree that were rough
enough for him to climb onto. Without further thought he
reached up and grasped a whorl just above his head. As if by
magic a ladder appeared attached to the trunk. Gleefully he
grasped a rung and stealthily climbed up into its branches
where he sat and waited. As he looked around he could see
the chocolate pear was easily within his grasp. Sitting next
to the pear was a bird. It appeared to be guarding the fruit.

Rebekkah meanwhile had started to run along the path where she had seen her brother disappear. This was such a lovely place and there was so much to see that she frequently became distracted; stopping to stroke an otter or a badger. It was a while before she got to the tree. Oblivious to her brother sitting above her she called out for him. No answer. But then something dropped on her shoulder making her jump. It was a dead bird. She screamed and looked around her. 'Jacob!' She shouted. 'Please come out, I don't want to play anymore.'

Silence.

She looked at the bird closely and gingerly touched it with her finger. It was still warm. It seemed odd and out of place. It marred the sense of paradise. She wasn't expecting to see death in this wonderful place. Then she saw him, perched above her. She cupped her hands over her eyes to get a better look. Shards of bright light stabbed their way through the leaves of the tree and hurt her eyes. Jacob was holding something in his hand. Something dark. And next to him, wound tightly around the branch was a yellow snake with red eyes. A shiver ran down her spine.

'Jacob,' she screamed, 'There's a snake next to you!'

Jacob slowly made his way down to her. Dropping the last metre he turned and looked at her, an odd gleam in his eye. Colouring slightly he wiped his mouth with the back of his hand. There were dark stains above his lips.

He reached into his pocket and pulled out what looked like a chocolate fruit. Hesitantly he offered her the dark thing. She looked past him and up into the tree. She was looking for the snake but it had gone. In its place were branches laden with chocolate covered apples. It reminded her of the Christmas tree at home laden with chocolate gifts. A memory flashed across her mind of both of them peeling the silver paper from the hanging chocolate bells one Christmas and eating all the chocolate baubles. Mum had taken their Christmas presents away for two whole days as a punishment.

'Jacob, what is this tree? Did the eagle tell you about the tree of knowledge of good and evil? We aren't to eat from it. How do you know what this tree is? You might have broken the eagle's rules.'

He grinned. 'Well, yes and you know what, that eagle lied, nothing has happened to me and this chocolate is lovely. I'd go so far as to say, 'heavenly' and he laughed an odd, lopsided laugh. 'Try some.'

Rebekkah backed away as if he was offering her a snake. 'You idiot', she shouted. 'You idiot; now you've ruined everything!'

'Aw come on Bekkah how can eating a little bit of scrumptious chocolate ruin everything? Hey! Did you have a hamper of food too? I had chip butties in mine. It was all my favourite food but there was no chocolate. I think the eagle likes a joke and we were meant to find this tree. She wants us to enjoy this place and do as we like. It's an adventure. This is a test to see if we are brave enough to take a risk. You like chocolate and she didn't say exactly what would happen to us, did she?'

Rebekkah looked at the chocolate. It was true she loved chocolate and she was very hungry. It seemed hours since she had eaten. What was it the eagle had said about this tree? She couldn't really remember. Jacob was so logical what he said made sense and she so wanted some chocolate. She reached out and took the piece he offered her and ate it. It tasted good. And then she waited. Nothing bad happened.

'Oh I feel sick now,' said Rebekkah.

She looked at Jacob who also looked a bit green. And then it happened. A shadow flew across the sun and the silhouette of a giant bird descended on them. They were grabbed in two mighty claws promptly lifted out of the nest and into the sky.

They flew like this for some way before the eagle descended and dropped them onto the ground. They both rolled some way before they came to a halt. She landed next to them and fixed her unblinking stare on them both.

'What did you do?' Jacob took one look at her, dropped to his knees and vomited up the contents of his stomach.

'Eeuuw.' Rebekkah screwed up her face, 'That stinks.' And promptly followed suit.

The eagle spoke to them both,

'Listen carefully to what I am about to say. You could have had anything you wanted in that perfect world of the nest but you were disobedient. You did the one thing you were told not to do. Jacob, you were tempted by greed and as a result allowed the snake to kill the bird guarding the fruit. Rebekkah, you too gave in to greed. You were unwise to listen to your brother. Now you are free once more but you can't go back to the nest until you have learnt to be less selfish.'

'Oh eagle,' sobbed Rebekkah. 'I am so sorry; it was Jacob he made me do it. I wasn't even sure if it was the tree of knowledge. Please give us another chance. I don't want to go home.'

Jacob, still crouching on all fours, said nothing.

The eagle looked from one child to another and then, picking them up more gently this time, flew up into the sky. As they flew it became darker and darker until at last they reached the outskirts of their town. Finally, the eagle hovered above their home. Bending her elegant neck she picked Jacob up by his collar and pushed him through the bedroom window. He collapsed onto the floor in a heap. Rebekkah was gently deposited on the window ledge and then nudged through the window with a push of the beak.

'Goodbye Rebekkah. I shall be with you always. We shall meet again.' And with that she was gone.

Rebekkah looked at her brother who was slowly getting to his feet.

'I'm going to bed,' he said gruffly. 'I'm tired.'

'Aren't we going to talk about what happened?' She demanded.

'Talk about what? There's nothing to talk about. Now get out of my room, you silly little twerp.' Jacob opened the door and shoved her onto the landing. His door closed with a click and she found herself looking at the smooth white painted surface. She raised her fists to bang on the door but then realised that this would wake her parents. Thinking better of it she headed into her own room, quickly undressed, took to her bed and slipped into an uneasy sleep full of dreams of snakes, dead birds and chocolate.

CHAPTER 10

MONDAY MORNING - REBEKKAH

Rebekkah opened her eyes and was overwhelmed by a sense of sadness. She squeezed her eyes shut and tried to re-enter her dream. As hard as she tried she could not get back to the joy of the nest. All she could see in her mind's eye was the rigid body of the dead bird. Tears ran down her face. What had they done? Jacob, it was Jacob's fault, he had ruined everything. Then almost simultaneously another thought ran through her head like an engine pulling a carriage of anxiety. It was Monday morning. School! Would Miss Bates be back or would they have the old battle-axe again? Groaning she pulled the covers over her head and tried to retreat into her own little world.

'Rebekkah! Get up!' her mother had grabbed the covers and pulled them off, dumping them on the floor. No time seemed to have passed in her world although Rebekkah figured they must have been at the nest for at least a day.

Breakfast was a silent affair. Neither child spoke. Jacob avoided looking at his sister and thankfully mum seemed preoccupied and was working on her iPad. Dad had gone to work early. It was a dull grey day; the sort that meant wet play. It mirrored their feelings. There would be no sun to brighten up their Monday morning.

On arriving at school her heart sank when she walked into the supply teacher, Miss Cannon. Menacingly she greeted her by name and said she was 'delighted' she would see her later in her lesson. She also demanded the homework that had been set and made Rebekkah stand in the classroom while she read it. On completion she screwed it up and threw it in the bin.

'That took me two hours to write.' Rebekkah was horrified.

'Really? Well it looked like it had taken you ten minutes. Do it again. And you will get more to do unless you change your attitude. Tie your hair back and tuck your shirt in. Do try in your lessons today. And remember, I shall be keeping my eye on you.'

Smarting with anger and humiliation, Rebekkah turned on her heels and walked away. She felt hatred welling up in her. She could taste it in her mouth. She wanted to slap the woman.

Freda was back. She sat on her own by the window reading her book. Rebekkah marched up to her. She was still angry and spoke harshly to the girl.

'I am never working with you again. You got me into big trouble on Friday with your stupid antics. No wonder no one ever wants to work with you. You are so lame and a loser.' The words just tumbled out of her mouth, all the venom that had built up poured over poor Freda. Rebekkah grabbed the girl's book. 'Did you hear what I said? Did you?' Freda lunged at her trying to grab the book. Enjoying the power, Rebekkah held it high over her head.

'Here Bekkah, over here, pass it to me.' More girls stopped what they were doing to watch.

The book flew through the air towards Amelia who dropped it. Screaming with rage Freda lunged at Amelia knocking over a chair. 'Don't! Don't! Give it back. GIVE, ME, IT, BACK!'

Rebekkah picked up the book. 'If you want it, come and get it. Or, are you going to run off again?'

Sobbing hysterically Freda snatched the book from Rebekkah's hand at the same moment as Miss Cannon appeared at the door. Rebekkah's heart sank; now she was for it. The woman surveyed the scene. Her lips were drawn in a thin, tight line that accentuated the moustache above. Her eyes, snake like, flickered from Freda to Amelia and then finally settled on Rebekkah. A memory flashed across Rebekkah's mind of Jacob offering her the chocolate fruit. She should have said no then she would still be in the nest rather than standing in front of this mean woman who clearly hated her.

'I see you have not learned your lesson from yesterday young lady so you will spend all your break and lunch times with me writing out copies of the school rules, in particular, the sections on bullying which you will write out in triplicate. Do you know what triplicate means?'

'Three times.' murmured Rebekkah.

'That's a relief because the next task was for you to write out the dictionary. We'll save that for the next time when you transgress. You can look that word up. Now girls, the entertainment is over; let's get ready for registration. Freda, get up and stop snivelling or go to the nurse.'

The morning passed without further incident but then a strange thing happened. Just before lunch the receptionist brought a note to Rebekkah informing her that she was not to get the bus home as her mother would collect her. She had an appointment with the Headmistress and it coincided with home time. She was to wait in reception. A feeling of unease settled on her. What was going on? Had Miss 'snake eyes' Cannon reported her for bullying? Would she be expelled? The sense of foreboding gathered momentum as the day developed until the final bell. Usually a happy child, Rebekkah's head drooped and after collecting her coat and bag she made her way to reception. As she sat on the large leather chair her eyes surveyed the panelled walls. It seemed that the past headmistresses of the school looked accusingly at her from their portraits while the ancient clock counted the seconds in tocks. And then she saw it. A glass case hung on the wall full of stuffed birds. In the centre was an eagle. It stood to attention, on a smooth branch, talons open and beak slightly ajar.

Rebekkah stood up and walked over to the case where she bent forward slightly so that she could look the bird in the eye. Feeling slightly dizzy, she wiggled her fingers in her ears and then rubbed her forehead. As her hands slipped over her eyes she was aware of a rushing sound and then sharp zigzags of light entered her vision blurring her view of the great bird. Her feet were lifted up and she tipped forward. The expected bang as she collided with the cabinet wall did not happen; instead the rushing noise grew louder and the zigzags faster. The orange eye of the eagle filled her vision; it was crowned with a hood of fur and stared unblinkingly at her.

Her body shifted horizontally and she headed towards the black lifeless pupil of the eye like a bullet. Terrified, she cried out as she was sucked into the dark void. What was going to happen? Would she hit the eagle's brain? The noise stopped as suddenly as it started and she dropped to the floor where she knelt and rested on all fours. Her head hung down and her mouth was open, panting in little gasps. The place was full of light, pure transparent light. She suddenly felt at peace. The burden of fear that she had carried on her back all day slipped away. She wanted to stay in this place forever.

'Rebekkah!' her mother's voice penetrated and cut through her thoughts; the light immediately evaporated and she found herself once more in the reception area. Her mother was kneeling next to her. She was lying flat on her back on the floor. Her mother's face was anxious.

'Hello Mum,' the words seemed to come from somewhere outside of her head; her voice was weird, small and thin as if she was a long way away and in a tunnel.

The Headmistress was with her mother; Rebekkah looked anxiously from one to the other. Was she in trouble? Her mother had clearly been crying. Her mascara usually so carefully applied was smudged. It made her look like a clown. Clumsily she got to her feet. Her mother helped her into a nearby chair. She was given some water and told to sit with her head between her knees. After a while she looked shyly up at the two adults who were standing nervously by her side. The Headmistress spoke first.

'Rebekkah dear, I am afraid we have to give you some bad news. Your mother has asked me to tell you that you will have to leave St Swithin's at the end of the month.'

'Why? Oh mum, I didn't mean to hurt Freda. I am sorry, I will make it up to her.'

Puzzled the head looked at her. 'Freda? I don't think she is the cause at all. Mrs Taylor, perhaps you should explain.'

Rebekkah looked at her mother who sniffed and dabbed at her eyes. 'Your father and I are separating. He has lost his job and we can't afford to pay the school fees.'

'But he was at work this morning,' Rebekkah's voice tailed off.

'Yes, he has been lying. He lost his job three months ago. He hasn't been paying your school fees. The first I knew of it was when the Headmistress called me in to talk about non-payment of fees. I then phoned him and he told me. He didn't want to tell us and so has been pretending to go to work. He has been unbearable to live with, I knew something wasn't right.'

'But what about me? Can't you pay the fees? Dad will get another job.'

Her mother looked at her. 'We are getting a divorce. I can't afford to live apart from your father and pay the fees. Something has to give. There's a good state school down the road, and you will get a good report from here.'

'Mum, that's mean. Dad needs you now.'

The Head stepped in. 'Now, now, Rebekkah there are some things that are difficult to understand but one day you will. You need to support your mother in her decision and please do not make life more difficult for her. I am sorry you are leaving as you have been a very good pupil but I am sure you will do well wherever you go to school.'

Rebekkah looked at her. One day she would just be a painting, a memory like the rest of the headmistresses on the wall. She would be reduced to oils on a canvas. What did she know? She did not even know what was going on in her own classrooms.

'And Jacob?' she asked 'What about Jacob?'

Her mother sighed. 'Your father is speaking to his headmaster.'

CHAPTER 11

MONDAY MORNING - JACOB

Jacob had also woken up feeling depressed. The memory of the events in the nest troubled him. He did not want to admit it to Rebekkah, but he felt guilty for the first time in his life. Pushing the unwanted thoughts away he rationalised the experience as a dream. No time had passed. He chose not to talk to Rebekkah because he wanted the thoughts to fade. It was with relief therefore when he climbed out of the car and walked away from her to the bus stop.

When Jacob got to school he was summoned to the Head's office where he was questioned about the bus incident. No, he did not know why he had done it. Yes, it had been a silly and immature thing to do. Yes, he was sorry for bringing the school into disrepute. No, it would not happen again. Yes, he would write a letter of apology. Yes, he would do it now. As he sat in the outer office he went to that place in his head where his lips and his thoughts were separate. He laughed out loud at the memory of the girl's squealing and the bus driver posting the little worms through the window.

When finished, he went to the toilets on the way back to the classroom taking an extra long time. It was only French.

On returning to his classroom, Jacob settled into his chair and stared out of the window. His thoughts turned to the nest. Not usually given to fanciful thoughts, he struggled with the vivid nature of his memories. He could still feel the rhythm of the eagle's wings beneath him. He really should drink more water, he thought to himself; he was just feeling a bit faint and dehydrated. Mum was always telling him to drink more. The boys around him were working steadily, heads bent, industriously focused on the essays they were writing. His gaze turned to the board where the teacher had written the task.

Racontez une histoire sur un aigle. (Tell a story about an eagle)

Was this some kind of a joke? Had the class agreed to play a trick on him while he was out of the room? He looked furtively around the room. Were they pretending to work? Was anyone trying to stifle a grin? Any moment now would they all simultaneously put down their pens and laugh at him? He looked around the room trying to catch the eye of his friend. It was not logical. He had not told anyone about the nest. And then, it came to him. Rebekkah must have been blabbing about the dream and somehow the boys had heard about it. The little twit! What was he to do now? Then the teacher's voice cut through his musings.

'Taylor, get on with your work, stop gazing around the room. Boys you have ten minutes left.'

No one was laughing. Slowly he sucked the pen and started leafing through his French dictionary. Painfully he began to write.

L'aigle est un grand oiseaux. Il habite dans un nid. He had to look up the words: big, bird, live, and nest. By the time he had worked out the verb endings the lesson was over. Subdued, he sat quietly at his desk.

'Hey Jay, what did the Hedgehog do to you?' Hedgehog was the nickname of the Headteacher, so named because of his spiky black hair. 'Rumour has it you've been expelled.'

'What? Nah, he's soft as putty. I had to write a grovelling letter to the bus company and that was it.'

'Are you sure?' persisted Nathan. 'Your dad was in earlier this morning, I saw him. He didn't look at all happy. I overheard him saying to the office lady that you'd be leaving by the end of this week.'

'What? That can't be right. Hedgehog didn't mention anything about me leaving or dad coming in.'

Nathan shrugged, 'Only saying what I heard and saw. I know your dad when I see him.'

'If you don't shut up, I'll make you', threatened Jacob. Nathan stuck his tongue out and ran off, half turning once he was at a safe distance. 'You are all talk Jacob Taylor. Go back to your worms.'

Jacob started to run and then thought better of it. Lunch was calling and he was hungry. Once in the dining hall he forgot his earlier disquiet and tucked into a huge plate of pasta and cheese. The dinner lady had tried to place something green on his plate but he had pulled it away before his dinner was contaminated. Then it happened. Mr Hedgehog appeared at the door looking for someone. He shaded his eyes against the glare of the sun, which always streamed in through the floor to ceiling windows at the end of the room. A tall man, he bent his head to speak to the dinner staff on duty who pointed straight at Jacob. Hedgehog nodded at Jacob and beckoned to him to follow him. Beads of sweat gathered on Jacob's forehead. Boys looked curiously at him. Nathan grinned and mouthed, 'I told you so.' Jacob ignored him, left his plate on the table and walked after the Headmaster.

It was cool and dark in the corridor. The tall man was standing in the door of a classroom. He beckoned to him to join him whereupon he shut the door.

'Now Jacob, there is no easy way to tell you this but your father came to see me this morning.'

Jacob looked up at him. 'I am afraid it's bad news. Your father has lost his job and is unable to continue paying your school fees. You are to leave at the end of this week.'

Jacob's heart missed a beat, his head thumped as a confusion of thoughts bombarded his brain. 'Dad hasn't lost his job; he went to work this morning. I don't believe you.' The boy's aggression tumbled out as he squared up to the Headmaster; a little David against the giant Goliath.

'Well, he came in before school; maybe he didn't tell you he was coming in to see me. I am sorry Jacob.'

'But you spoke to me this morning, told me to write a letter of apology, how does that fit? You didn't say anything then?'

'No I didn't. I did know when I spoke to you but chose not to tell you until you had written the letters. You aren't an easy pupil, Jacob. I did not think you would apologise if you knew you were leaving. I have to put the interests of my school first. I can't have boys creating chaos on a bus and just let it go. You are a difficult young man. A word of advice; a new school offers a new start. Take it.'

Jacob looked at the man. His lip curled, 'you are an idiot. I'm glad I'm leaving, this is a rubbish school anyway.'

'Go to the reflection room Jacob. And I shall get your father to come and collect you. You are suspended for the remainder of the time that you have left here.'

The journey home took place in silence. Finally, they pulled up in the drive. His father pulled the hand brake on rather too viciously and then turned to him.

'Jacob, I can't be doing with your rudeness and selfishness right now. This is not a good time for me. I have been made redundant and so money is tight. That's why I have to take you out of your school. To be honest you haven't made the most of the opportunity and I think a state school might do you some good.'

Jacob looked at him. His mind was full to the brim of thoughts darting about his head like little fish in shallow water. Dad, a normally confident and aloof man, now seemed weak and empty, deflated like a balloon that had been forgotten after the Christmas festivities were long gone. Instead of pity Jacob felt an arrow of anger strike his heart. He thought of the humiliation he had felt when Hedgehog had informed him of his father's predicament.

'Why didn't you tell me? Why did you leave that idiot to tell me? It was so embarrassing. And he tricked me. Stupid man, I had to write a letter to that bus company and all the time he was secretly laughing at me knowing I was leaving.' The more he thought about it, the more angry he became. His fists were balls in his hands and his chin jutted out belligerently.

His father's eyes narrowed. 'As usual it's all about you, Jacob isn't it? I had hoped for a bit more maturity. A bit more understanding but no, here we are again. On the planet called me. I wanted to tell you in a different way but you might as well hear it now. Your mother and I are separating and you will live with me. So, you had better start being a bit more thoughtful, my lad.'

Jacob fumbled for the door handle and yanked it open. He pulled open the back door and grabbed the handles on his school bag. His eyes were clouded by tears, his nose blocked and he wanted to sniff but that would have been weak. So, he quickly turned away and marched into the house where he hid in the familiar darkness of his bedroom.

CHAPTER 12

REBEKKAH'S NEW SCHOOL

The following Monday came too quickly for Rebecca and not quickly enough for Jacob. He and Dad had moved into a small flat while Rebecca had stayed in the family home with Mum. This seemed unfair to Jacob even though he marginally preferred his father to his mother. He liked his bedroom in the old house. It had been his haven on many occasions. At least living with Dad meant he got to eat the food that he liked. Dad ate takeaways and loved his fat and sugar whereas Mum always insisted on fruit and healthy food. Rebecca was secretly quite glad at the way things had turned out. Seeing less of her big brother was a bonus and although sorry to say goodbye to her friends, she was glad to see the back of Miss Cannon. By the end of the week both children would wish they had never been born.

For Rebekkah it started on Thursday. The first three days had gone well. The other girls in her class seemed friendly enough and wanted to be her friend. Her new class teacher was delighted with her. She found most subjects easy and discovered that she was way ahead in maths and reading.

Eager to please and to make a good impression, her hand was constantly in the air. Gradually the atmosphere in the class began to change. Other students exchanged looks when she answered a question and made faces behind her back. Then, it happened, Rebekkah was asked to read out her English homework.

'Dreams,' she said in her loudest reading voice. She stood up and breathed deeply just as she had been taught in public speaking class.

'I dream a great deal. Last night I dreamt I was standing in a field of hay. It had been gathered into bales by the farmer and stacked, ready for animal feed. There were thirty bales altogether. Then, an odd thing happened. One by one the bales of hay grew legs and jumped down from the stack and surrounded me in the middle of the field. Once complete they formed themselves into a circle and bowed down to me.' Rebekkah stopped and looked up. The entire class were staring at her. They were completely silent. Then the teacher spoke. 'That's very interesting Rebekkah. Sounds like you might be Prime Minister or something one day. Wouldn't surprise me at all, you are brainier than this lot put together. Darren, can you read out your work please? And then it's time to get ready for swimming.'

In the changing rooms a small group of girls huddled together by the lockers. Rebekkah got changed quickly as she loved swimming and wanted to be first in the pool. She gathered up her clothes and tried to open the locker door to put her clothes away but a large girl with wonky teeth stood in her way.

'Excuse me, Kirsty,' she spoke politely.

'Excuse me, Kirsty,' sneered the girl as she mimicked Rebekkah's posh accent. 'Why, what you done? Did yer make a smell? I can smell a bad smell can't you girls?' The others gathered round. Some smiled menacingly, others pushed to see what was going on.

'Please, could you just let me get to the locker?'

'Yes of course, ma'am, anything you say ma'am.' Kirsty stood to one side and then, as Rebekkah bent down to put her things inside, grabbed her bag and gave her a hefty shove. Rebekkah fell. Two more girls got down next to her and manhandled her into the locker and shut the door.

'So, geeky girl, if you think you are so smart, get yourself out of there.' There was a squeal of laughter and then lots of giggling. After a while it became quiet as the girls drifted off to the pool.

It was dark inside the locker. It smelt of stinky socks and shoes. She tasted panic in the back of her throat. She began to hammer on the door.

'Please let me out. Oh please let me out.' No one came. She began to hammer wildly against the door. Panic flooded over her, tears poured down her face and her nose ran. 'What if she used up all the oxygen and died of suffocation? What if she was left here over night? She could not breathe. Her thoughts turned to Jacob - logical, rational Jacob. He would not panic he would say something scientific like: sit still, calm down and take deep breaths. Thoughts of her brother made her feel desperately homesick. Her life was falling apart. What had she done wrong? Then she felt it. She became aware of a presence with her in the locker which seemed to expand and fill the entire space, but then grew and grew until the back of the locker disappeared altogether and she could see a beautiful field. Unsteadily, she stood up and walked out into the fresh air where a beautiful golden eagle was waiting for her.

'Rebekkah, climb on my back. I am getting you out of here.' Joyfully she ran to the eagle and buried her head in its rich soft downy feathers. 'Oh eagle. Is it really you? Can you help me?' The eagle reached over to her and gently stroked her hair with its long hooked beak. 'I can't stay long but I want to show you something.' Rebekkah climbed onto her back and together they soared up into the deep blue sky. Up, up they went until the top of a mountain came into view. The eagle circled it several times and then dropped down onto the flat stones. She arched her back and stretched her wings before folding them carefully so as not to hurt Rebekkah.

'It's so beautiful,' said Rebekkah. 'Yes,' replied the eagle. 'Never forget that despite your broken dreams it is still a beautiful world. You must be strong Rebekkah, and humble.'

'Oh eagle, it's hard. Everything is changing. Dad, Mum, Jacob, school and those girls were so mean.'

The eagle looked at her with her unblinking orange eyes. 'And it will continue but there are a few on your side. Jealousy is a powerful emotion, Rebekkah. Things will get worse before they get better. You must be brave. Now take one last look at the view and then we must go.'

There was a grinding sound and then the locker door flew open. A girl that Rebekkah knew from her class was standing there. She looked furtively around. 'Come on. Get out and be quick about it before the others come.' She thrust a bag at Rebekkah as she crawled out of the space.

'Thank you', stammered Rebekkah. 'I will never forget this.' The girl looked at her. 'Don't say anything to the others and keep your mouth shut.' She then turned and walked away leaving Rebekkah to get dressed. Panicking Rebekkah dressed quickly. She was late for her lesson and she hated being late. Grabbing her bag she shoved her feet into her shoes, jamming her heel down on the back of the shoe and half-walked, half-ran, down the corridor. She burst into the classroom and gasped out a 'sorry miss for being late.'

The class tittered and Rebekkah caught Kirsty looking at her. She mouthed, 'Don't say a thing, or else.'

The teacher was staring at her. 'Rebekkah what have you done to your shirt? Did they not teach you how to button a blouse at that independent school of yours?'

'She probably had a servant to dress her,' sneered a girl with a big nose and dyed orange hair. The class roared with laughter. With a pang of embarrassment Rebekkah realised that they had been waiting for her humiliation and were glad. Tears stung her eyes; she looked helplessly at the teacher. She did not want to go down in her estimation, she had been taught that teachers were kind and fair and if you told the truth against bullies they would help you. But then a vision of Miss Cannon floated before her eyes. She found herself looking for the girl who had released her but she was nowhere to be seen.

'Well Rebekkah, I had thought more of you than this but in the light of an inadequate explanation I am going to have to place you in detention. You will have lunch and then return to the classroom where I shall set you some jobs. The hamster needs a clean out and you can pick the chewing gum off the bottom of the desks. Be grateful I am not going to make you eat it.'

The class laughed again. Rebekkah dropped her head and slipped into her seat, cheeks aflame with embarrassment. She began to re-button her shirt as the lesson continued and attention turned away from her to the board. For the rest of the day she kept her head down and answered no further questions. As she walked to the bus Kirsty pushed up behind her. 'Well done, geek, at least you aren't a snitch as well as a show off. But don't think I'm finished with you yet. I don't like you. You need to get in tomorrow early and do my homework for me. Got that? 8 o'clock, be in the dining hall.'

'But my mum doesn't drop me off until 8.30.'

Kirsty put her face up very close to Rebekkah's; she could smell stale breath and school on the bigger girl. 'I don't care. Tell her you have a club or something; make it up. Use that brain of yours. Just do it or else something worse will happen to you.' With that she popped a bubble gum into her mouth, grinned and walked off.

Feeling miserable, Rebekkah climbed onto the bus, settled into a window seat, pulled her school bag onto her knee and stared out of the window. What was happening to her? Her nice safe world had turned upside down. It all seemed to stem from the nest. Was the eagle friend or foe? Was the bird real? Sometimes she seemed as real as Jacob and at other times just a fantasy. She could not make sense of it all. She leaned against the bus window, which was misted with breaths and steamy coats. It was raining heavily outside. She drew a bird into the haze in front of her and then with a swipe of her hand rubbed it away. The eagle was like that.

CHAPTER 13

JACOB'S NEW SCHOOL

Jacob's week started well. He had looked forward to Monday morning. It had been boring at home with just his dad for company and he was glad to get out and into a new environment. No school was going to be as bad as St Michael's. On arrival at the school he had been greeted by the Head of Year and taken to his new form. A couple of lads had been told to be his buddy but it was clear they had not wanted to do it and after taking him to the tuck shop at break, they had just disappeared. Jacob didn't mind; they were dull anyway. They did not know anything about black holes and quarks. It did not for one moment occur to him that they might have found him boring. Such self-awareness was beyond Jacob.

He quickly adapted to the subjects he enjoyed - science and maths. Thankfully most of the boys hated French as much as he and religious education did not seem to exist at all. They had some subject called citizenship that most people messed about in, so that was all right. PE was a bit of an endurance test; Jacob was not sporty and slightly on the tubby side. He hated contact sports with a passion and was inclined to be uncoordinated. Usually he was not picked for teams and the other boys moaned and groaned when the sports teacher put him on their side. Jacob did not want to be on anyone's side especially not in rugby. Within five minutes of the start of the game he had allowed himself to be tripped up whereupon he pretended to bang his head, an old trick. Then, complaining of a headache he was told to sit on the bench. This was a much better place to be than in a game of rugby, he thought smugly to himself.

He somehow got to the end of Thursday without upsetting any teacher or drawing too much attention to himself. He got good marks in his work and it seemed as if he had made the adjustment successfully. He and dad were getting on better too although his father still seemed disinterested in what he was up to, spending long hours on the computer which was fine by Jacob. Then, it happened.

It was Friday morning. The sky was dark and heavy with rain clouds. Jacob noticed how dreary everything was in the rain. The wind howled around him, a single blast nearly knocked him off his feet. A half empty can of lager dribbled a dark liquid onto the path as it rolled back and forth in the wind. He kicked it, covering his shoe in stickiness. He grinned to himself; he would smell like a brewery. As he hitched his rucksack onto his shoulders he noticed a commotion on the street in front of him. Getting closer he could see two lads surrounded by a group of boys. One was dangling a mobile phone high above a small boy's head and, as he jumped up to take it from him, the older boy threw it to someone in the crowd. The owner darted uselessly over to the recipient just in time to see the phone fly through the air again and land in the hands of another boy. He was getting desperate. Jacob felt sorry for him and waded in. He intercepted the phone as it flew through the air and handed it to the small child who muttered a 'thanks' and quickly tucked the precious item into his pocket and ran off. Angry, the lads turned on him.

'Who do you think you are, posh boy?'

'Suppose you think you are better than the rest of us.'

'Who told you to interfere, mister high and mighty.'

Jacob was shoved and pushed. He looked around him for the lad whose phone he had saved but he was nowhere to be seen. He held his hands up and reasoned,

'Look he was only a small kid. He was on his own, there are loads of you.'

'Yeah but you're not though are you?' sneered a big lad. 'There's quite a bit of you,' and he took a swing at Jacob punching him in the stomach. Jacob doubled up in pain. There was a laugh and then another boy grabbed his bag and dumped the contents on the ground. His iPad was grabbed and that was the last Jacob saw of it. He had no idea who had taken it. Furious he swung blindly at the nearest boy. His hand caught the lad on the chin and he fell to the ground. Gasping he turned and crouched like a tiger, eyes narrowed in pain, breath coming in short gasps.

'Give me back my iPad,' he yelled, much to the amusement of the boys surrounding him. Then a cry went up, 'Quick! Scarper, teacher's coming;' the crowd melted away leaving Jacob next to the boy whom he had knocked out.

The teacher had a radio grasped in his hand and was speaking urgently into it. As he reached Jacob he yelled at him to stand still and then dropped to his knees to check out the unconscious boy.

'You'll be in big trouble for this. What have you done?'

Jacob began to pick up his things. 'It wasn't my fault; I was attacked first. And they've got my iPad.'

'Go to the cooler and wait for me there.'

'Why? It's not my fault. It's them who should be in the cooler. Didn't you hear me, they have got my iPad?' Jacob was now shaking uncontrollably with the injustice of the situation. His iPad was his most precious possession.

The teacher shouted at him, 'Go to the cooler. Now! You don't want to get into any more trouble than you are already.'

Jacob looked at him. Rage overwhelmed him. He shouted, 'This is a horrible school; I hate you and everyone in it. You are all idiots.' Picking up his bag he ran towards the school gate and out onto the road. He didn't look back.

CHAPTER 14

REBEKKAH AND KIRSTY

Rebekkah's Friday was also going badly. When she had told her mother that she needed to be at school for eight o'clock, Mrs Taylor had gone into meltdown. No, she could not get Rebekkah into school at that time. She had a meeting arranged at nine. Did Rebekkah not understand that she was organising her time around her for this week? She could not just shift everything around at the last minute.

Rebekkah had then burst into tears and yelled at her mother. Did she not understand how hard it was starting a new school? She missed her friends and was trying to make new ones. This was a club she wanted to attend. At that point her mother had softened and agreed to take her earlier. However things had not gone to plan. Mum had received a phone call from Dad just as they were about to leave the house that left her grumpy and irritable. Rebekkah had been hopping from one foot to the next mouthing 'hurry up' at her mother who had clenched her teeth in anger and waved her away. Now she was rushing through the gates at ten past eight.

She arrived in the dining hall; her face red with the exertion of running through the school with a heavy bag and stood anxiously at the door looking for Kirsty.

'So there you are,' muttered a voice in her ear. She jumped. Kirsty must have been hiding in a nearby classroom, as she had not been there seconds before.

'You are late, geek. No one makes me wait. I've got a punishment lined up for you but for now let's get this homework done.' She dragged Rebekkah by the arm into a classroom and got out her books.

'Maths first, let me see your work,' she demanded. Rebekkah reached into her bag and produced her exercise book and opened it at the right page. Kirsty quickly scribbled down the answers. 'Now English, blimey, you've written a lot,' she moaned, 'this will take me ages to copy.'

She thought for a minute and then made a decision. 'We don't have English until this afternoon. I'm not copying all that out. You will type it up for me on the computer, you should have thought about this yourself, you selfish girl. And then you can print it out and give it to me.'

'But,' stammered Rebekkah, 'our work will be the same.'

'No it won't,' grinned Kirsty, 'Cos you are going to do a new one for yourself.'

'But I won't have time. I have detention at lunchtime. Remember? You made me late by locking me in that locker.

Now I have to pick chewing gum off desks. Probably you put it there in the first place.' Her words tumbled out in a rush. She had not meant to speak so forcefully. Something instinctively told her that the bigger girl would punish her for her insolence. Sure enough, Kirsty thrust her face into Rebekkah's and hissed, 'No? Well that's your problem. You should have thought about this last night. In future you write two pieces of work. One for you and one for me or else worse will happen to you. The locker was just the beginning. Get it?' With that she stuffed her books back in her bag and strode off.

Now wretchedly downcast, Rebekkah checked her watch noting it was already time for registration. She repacked her bag and headed off to her form room. The girls inside were laughing and joking. They ignored her completely. She felt tears welling up in the back of her eyes. Turning her head away she dropped into her seat and opened a book. She had never felt so lonely.

Registration was a rushed affair. Their form teacher was apparently away and the very flustered Head of Year bustled in loudly exclaiming that they were late for assembly and needed to get a move on. Rebekkah suddenly felt a shaft of hope. If the teacher was not here then maybe the detention would be cancelled and she could do the homework. She waited behind after everyone had gone. The teacher was just finishing adding absence marks to the computer.

'Yes?' he looked at Rebekkah expectantly.

'Please Sir, I have a detention at lunch time with our Form Tutor, will it be rearranged when she comes back or do I still need to come here at lunch time?'

'Mmm, you are the new girl aren't you? In detention already? What did you do?'

Rebekkah had not expected an inquisition. 'Er, I lost my shoes in PE and so was late for her lesson.' she said rather lamely. She could not look the teacher in the eye and shuffled awkwardly from one foot to another.

'Ah,' said the man looking at her. 'Rebekkah it can be hard starting a new school. There's a lot to take in, new routines and so on. I will speak to your tutor when she gets back and say you were keen to do the detention. We will sort it out. Don't worry for today. Now better get yourself to assembly.' With that he logged out of the computer and dashed off.

His kindness comforted Rebekkah and sustained her until lunchtime. She decided to miss lunch and get the extra homework done. She did not want to get into any more trouble. Afternoon registration was less rushed. The register was called and the students were quiet. It was therefore really noticeable when the Head of Year appeared and asked for Rebekkah. Turning pink she got up from her desk and began to make her way towards him.

'Bring your bag Rebekkah,' he said. 'You won't be attending lessons this afternoon.' Turning back to collect her bag she caught Kirsty's eye.

'Say nothing, or else,' mouthed the girl.

Mystified and a bit scared, she followed the man out of the room and down the corridor. He paused and shortened his step so he could walk beside her.

'Rebekkah,' he said very solemnly, 'I have some bad news, your brother Jacob has gone missing. Your mum is waiting for you in my office, she wants you to be together with your father and the police would like to interview you.'

'What about?' she asked anxiously.

'To see if you have any idea about where he might have gone.'

Her first feeling was of relief that she would escape from school for the afternoon. Then she felt guilty. What if something terrible had happened to her brother? Although she did not like him very much he was still her brother. As these thoughts tumbled through her mind they arrived at the Head of Year's office where her mother was waiting. Her eyes were streaked with tears and she looked worried.

'Oh Bekkah!' She jumped up and threw her arms around her daughter. Rebekkah, unaccustomed to such a display of affection felt hugely embarrassed but nonetheless allowed herself to be entwined by her mother's skinny arms. Her body, bony and thin wasn't very comforting. Rebekkah shifted in her grasp and pushed her mother away.

'Where's Jacob, Mum?'

Her mother burst into tears, the Head of Year swiftly moved to the table and deftly passed her a box of tissues.

'We don't know. He has run away.'

CHAPTER 15

JACOB AT THE FACTORY

Jacob gazed at the derelict factory in front of him. It would be a good place to hide. Besides he was getting wet. It had not stopped raining since he had run away from school three hours before. He pulled up the hood on his thin soggy jacket and squinted right and left before sprinting across to the grey building. He circumnavigated it; occasionally jumping up to get a better look at a boarded up window. At last, he found what he was looking for: a window that had been forced open by a previous visitor. Hunting around for something to stand on, his eyes settled on a crate. Giving little thought to the possibility that someone else had already used this method of entry, he dragged it across to the window. He climbed onto the crate and then leapt goat like onto the large grey pockmarked window ledge. Perched like a brave little blackbird oblivious to the cat that waited underneath the tree, he scanned the drop below him. If only he could fly! He thought to himself. Taking a deep breath, he jumped. Landing awkwardly on his ankle he felt a sharp pain shoot up his leg. Damn, he had sprained something, but hopefully not broken. How was he to get out again? The window was way above him and there was no friendly crate on this side of the window. His ankle was throbbing and he could not see. He shunted across the floor on his bottom, wincing at the pain. He was aware of dust and dirt sticking to his wet trousers. His mother would be mad at him. The place was full of shadows; was that something sitting in the corner looking at him? Where was the door? Fear gnawed at his stomach. Dreadful thoughts tumbled through his mind. Stop it! Stop, It! He shouted to himself. A shaft of sunlight burst through the broken window illuminating the room. There was a door just in front of him. Jacob shuffled as fast as he could towards it. He levered himself up onto his left knee, his right foot extended to one side. Panting with the exertion he grabbed the handle and pulled. The door sprang open. It took a while for his eyes to adjust to the gloom of another dark room. It stank. What was that smell? He had come across it once before when in his uncle's garage. His uncle shot birds, mainly magpies. Dirty vermin, he had called them. Once they had fallen from the sky he would grab them by their feet and throw them in a sack. If one happened to still be alive he would slap its head against a nearby fence post before dumping it. He had left this sack of black feathery death in the shed, waiting for his next bonfire when he would burn the birds. Fascinated, Jacob had poked the sack with a stick and nearly gagged when thousands of little maggots wriggled out of the hole and onto the floor. The smell was the same.

He sat very still and waited for his eyes to adjust. To his right he could just make out a mound of something. A thought popped into his head. Why had not he considered this before he had jumped down from the window? What an idiot. He had been so intent on finding a place to hide that he had not given this a moment's thought. He was not the first to jump through. In fact someone else must have forced the window open. How had they got out? Perhaps they had not. Perhaps they were trapped, like him, and had died here. Perhaps this was the smell and it was coming from the mound. Or, perhaps the person was still here. Perhaps there were two and one had killed the other? His boyish imagination, fed by countless games of ghouls and werewolves, was now in overdrive: 'Oh God help me. I'll be next!'

The mound moved. This is it, thought Jacob. I am going to die. A voice came from the mound. Jacob looked around for something with which to defend himself. He saw a plank of wood and started shuffling towards it. The mound suddenly grew feet and arms and a head. A man stood before him. His face had an oily streak across the cheek, his matted hair was grey, he was dirty but despite this his eyes were deep set and infinitely blue. Jacob stared at him.

'Don't hurt me please. I meant no harm.'

'Why are you here boy?' the man's voice was deep. It reminded Jacob of a game he had once played with Dad when they had tried a variety of voices in a cave to see which was the loudest. The thought of Dad made him want to cry.

'I fell through the window.'

Vicki Gibson

'Mmm, I heard the noise. You alone?' Jacob started to say, yes, but then remembered the danger he was in. 'Yes, but I was playing hide and seek and there are others outside.'

'Yeah right,' there was a pause and then he continued, 'no school then?'

Jacob panicked, thinking quickly. 'No, we had a day off, you know a training day.' Lying was surprisingly easy; survival instinct was kicking in.

The man looked at Jacob for a long time. 'So, there's more of you eh? Well, I can't hear them, I think they must have gone and left you. Popular boy are you?'

Jacob was aware of how vulnerable he felt. He was standing like an ostrich on one leg. He knew he could not possibly make a run for it. 'Sometimes'.

'Ah' responded the man, 'so you aren't! A bit too cocky and sure of yourself are you? Other lads don't like that. What's your favourite subject?'

'Science,' said Jacob without hesitation. If he could keep the man talking then maybe he would be safe.

'Science,' mused the man. 'So, you don't believe in magic.'

'Magic is all based on illusion,' Jacob was on home territory here.

The man looked at him. 'What if I could show you some magic that you can't explain?'

Jacob looked at him. 'I might not be able to explain it straightaway but I'd work it out.'

'Come and sit next to me,' the man patted the floor. Jacob hesitated; he did not want to get too near the guy, the smell was bad enough from where he was. Also he was not sure what he was going to do.

'I'd rather stay over here, if you don't mind,' he said as politely as he could.

The man laughed, 'If I don't mind. What a polite boy you are. You aren't really in a position to refuse to do anything. So please yourself, sit down there and I will sort out that ankle of yours.' He turned away from Jacob and rummaged in the sack clothes that had been his bed a moment before. He found what he was looking for and approached Jacob. He had a tin in his hand. Kneeling beside the lad he gently touched his ankle, removed his shoe and then applied some foul smelling ointment to Jacob's foot. A deep heat squeezed its way between Jacob's skin and into his ankle. The ligaments, swollen and torn were engulfed by throbbing waves of energy. Jacob yelled in agony, swore at the man and pulled his foot away from the agonising touch.

'You idiot,' he shouted.

The man looked at him, 'You use that word a lot Jacob.'

Jacob scooted into the corner cradling his ankle in his hands: 'what have you done to my ankle? And how do you know my name? Who are you?'

The man was rocking on his feet. 'Things are not always what they seem Jacob. You think, because of the pain that something bad has happened to your ankle but have you tried walking on it?'

Jacob stared at him and then at his ankle. It was still throbbing but the pain was lessening. Gingerly he wriggled his toes and then moved the foot from side to side. It felt strong. He stretched out his leg and then carefully put some weight on it. Again, it felt strong despite the heat which lingered deep within the bone.

'How did you do that?' he whispered.

'Ah, that is for me to know and you to explain.' Just at that moment the door at the end of the warehouse was flung open. Jacob jumped. Standing silhouetted against the light was another man.

'What's going on here? Who's this? You kidnapped a boy? I just go out for an hour and come back to find you have a boy in tow. This could be our lucky day.' The man ambled up to Jacob and leered at him. Jacob shrank back in disgust, his breath smelt of fags and beer.

The healer, as he now became known in Jacob's head, pushed the newcomer away and marched him down to the end of the room. The two men huddled close together and seemed to be arguing. Jacob looked at the open door considering whether his ankle was now strong enough to make a run for it.

The first man came back. 'What's your parents' phone number Jacob? We want to phone home and let them know you are safe.'

Jacob looked from one to another. There was something odd about them. The second man was grinning and licking his lips. The first man would not look Jacob in the eye. Jacob felt very uncomfortable. But surely it could not do any harm to give them Dad's mobile number.

'0789567234,' he said. 'Can I speak to my dad please?'

'In a minute,' said the healer. 'Now give us your mobile.'

Jacob reluctantly handed it over. The man squinted as he punched in the numbers. He had a fleck of white saliva at the edge of his mouth as he raised the phone to it.

'Hello, is that Jacob's dad? Yeah? Just to let you know we have your son and if you want to see him alive you need to pay us ten thousand pounds by tonight.' Jacob's mouth dropped open. The person on the other end replied and the man offered the phone to Jacob. 'Tell him that it's true and that you are okay.'

Jacob took the phone, 'Hello dad? Yes, it's me. Yes it's true. I am in a warehouse...' The phone was snatched away from him and the man spoke into it. 'So, that was your son, now let's make arrangements for the transfer of money. Ten thousand pounds, no police and your son is returned to you safe and sound. You tell the police and you will only see your son in a box. Get it? You get the money and when you are ready phone me again on the number I am going to text you. It's a pay phone and you can't trace it. We will arrange an exchange.' He terminated the call with a flourish.

'I am so good at this kidnapping lark; I think I might make a habit of it.' He laughed and strode to the back of the warehouse where he produced some ropes. Kneeling in front of Jacob he tied his hands and feet together. 'Don't want you running off now do we?' He surveyed his handiwork and then turned to the healer who was standing watching him. He tossed him a beer and told him to settle down and wait for the call. The healer said nothing but took the beer and sat down a little distance from Jacob.

****

The school had already alerted Mr Taylor to his son's disappearance. He was not best pleased as he had an interview for a job that morning. He was in the middle of ironing his shirt when the phone rang. 'Flipping selfish kid,' he thought to himself.

Certain that Jacob was just attention seeking, he finished ironing his shirt and then tried to phone his son. Unsurprisingly Jacob failed to answer. Mr Taylor could well imagine his irritating son laughing to himself as he saw his father's number come up on the screen. He decided not to waste any more time and instead sent him a text message to phone home. Muttering to himself, he pulled on a jacket and tried to phone his wife as he made his way to the bus stop. She too was irritated by Jacob's disappearance but blamed her husband. Apparently he was not providing his son with the emotional support he needed. This had evolved into a full-scale argument about who was going to try and find Jacob when he had a job interview to prepare for and she had an important meeting that she could not possibly miss. Angry, he determined to ground Jacob for a month once he came home.

He went through the motions of the interview. It was at a lower level than he had been used to and the salary was also lower but he needed the work. He looked at his phone. There was still no message from Jacob. A niggle of anxiety touched his heart. What if something happened to him? Why had he run away? He phoned the school and asked for a meeting with the Head of Year who was concerned to hear that Jacob was still missing and suggested he call the police. Mr Taylor was shocked. He was unaccustomed to taking much notice of his son's antics; his policy had always been to ignore any bad behaviour in the hope that it and Jacob would go away. Sending him to his room seemed to work well and it got him out of his hair. So, the suggestion that he should call the police seemed a bit extreme. And then his phone rang. It was Jacob. Thank goodness. Relief quickly turned to anxiety as the rough voice on the other end told him that he had kidnapped his son. Every parent's nightmare suddenly became a reality. Guilt overwhelmed him. Why had he not taken this more seriously? He was in an agony of indecision. Should he phone the police?

****

Jacob felt sick and shaky. He was shivering with fear. The smell was really getting to him and he was not sure how much longer he could last without throwing up. He did not want to show weakness but he also wanted to cry and above all he wanted his dad. He caught the healer's eye.

'Why did you help me when you also planned to hurt me?' he asked.

'Shut up,' shouted the man from the back of the warehouse. 'You speak again and I'll stamp on your mouth.'

The healer walked over to him and bent down to check the ropes, as he did so he slipped Jacob a broken piece of glass. The other man stood up and half ran over to Jacob. He looked suspiciously at the two of them and also checked the ropes. As he bent his dark head over Jacob's feet and checked his wrists Jacob thought again of a magpie. His eyes were small and closely set. His nose was long and thin, tapering to a beak like end. Thin lips barely covered his tobacco stained, misshapen teeth. Jacob physically recoiled from the smell of his breath. 'What's up boy?' he cawed, pushing his face up against Jacob, 'part of me hopes your daddy don't come up with the money 'cos I'd enjoy cutting off your finger and sending it to him.' In his mind's eye Jacob suddenly thought of the eagle. He imagined the bird swooping down upon the magpie and grabbing him with her strong talons. In his dream the strong, honourable bird took the dark headed vermin to a dustbin, having dropped it into a box and shut the lid. Despite himself he found himself praying; 'Oh eagle, if you exist, please help me.'

The healer spoke in his deep sonorous voice, 'that's enough, leave the lad alone, can't you see he's terrified.' He placed his hand on the magpie's shoulders, pulling him backwards. The man yelled in fury and swung out at the healer hitting him square on the chin. The healer staggered backwards and collapsed onto the floor. Seizing his opportunity, Jacob began furiously working at the ropes using the shard of glass. Magpie picked up an iron bar and stood over the healer.

'First, I am going to kill you and then I am going to take all the money I get for this little geek myself.'

****

Mr Taylor turned the phone over in his hand. What should he do? He had seen these things happen in films and had always felt irritated with the victims. It seemed so obvious you should call the police. But now he was in the situation himself he was not so sure. And then, it happened. There was a knock at the door. Two female police officers stood before him. How did they know? Had not the man said he was not to tell the police? They explained that the school had contacted them and they wanted to take a few details. He found himself explaining about the phone call. They immediately became very grave and serious. One got straight onto the phone while the other asked for a picture of Jacob. His wife was called. She was to go to the school to see if Rebekkah might have any idea as to where Jacob might be. He was sitting with his head in his hands when she and

Rebekkah both arrived. She had whirled in demanding to be given an update and then had burst into tears. He reached out a tentative hand expecting rejection but instead she buried her head in his shoulder and sobbed. For the first time in months he held her and a bridge was built.

****

Jacob sawed at the ropes as if his life depended on it. He watched with deepening horror as the magpie swung an iron bar at the healer. It came crashing down onto the floor with a loud bang as the healer rolled out of the way and rugby tackled him to the floor. The magpie swore and struck out at the healer's head with the bar hitting him on the side of his shoulder. The man cried out in pain and then rolled sideways. Jacob sawed more urgently at his wrist. His thumb and finger were bleeding as the sharp glass cut into his flesh but he was making progress. He could feel no pain as one by one the entwined bits of braid frayed and popped. Finally, they dropped away from his wrists and he frantically set to work on his feet. He glanced fearfully at the writhing bodies and began to shuffle away from them towards the door working hard at the same time. He was aware of loud yells, shouts and screams. The magpie was now standing over the healer and raining blows down on his head and body, kicking him in the groin and head. The healer was curled in a foetal position trying to protect himself from the bombardment. The magpie turned and looked at where Jacob had been and with a shout of fury picked up the bar and ran after Jacob who by this point had reached the door. Absolutely terrified, Jacob clambered to his feet and clawed at the handle desperately trying to open it. The magpie grabbed his hand and twisted it behind his back. Instinctively Jacob stabbed at the man's face and neck with the shard. Howling in pain the man let go of Jacob to protect his eyes. Then, as if resurrected from the dead, the healer emerged out of the gloom and hurled himself on top of the magpie shouting at Jacob to run. Jacob grabbed the door handle and yanked it open. Finding himself in a cool, dark room he slammed the door behind him and wedged a substantial lump of wood under the handle. Grateful for fresh air, he gulped it into his lungs and hopped, feet together as fast as he could away from the door.

Adrenaline fuelled, he seemed possessed of super human energy. He could feel that the airflow was becoming stronger and he figured that there must be an exit at the end of it. Groping his way along the wall, his fingers found an old sign with the letters 'E it' on it and an arrow pointing left. There were now loud banging noises coming from the locked door. Sobbing with exertion and fear Jacob hopped in the direction of the arrow and then with relief found the door. He pushed against it and it flew open releasing him into a large yard. He dropped to his knees and rolled onto his back hugging his legs to his chest and panting with exhaustion. As he moved his head from side to side, his eye was drawn to a heap of rubbish in the corner of the yard. He was sure he could see a rusty old saw. He rolled back up and hopped over to the pile. The saw made quick work of the remaining ropes and as the last thread was broken he staggered to his feet and ran towards the stairs at the end of the yard. Emerging at the top he found himself in a busy street, he grabbed the nearest person, begging them for help and passed out.

CHAPTER 16

JACOB RETURNS TO SCHOOL

When Jacob opened his eyes he was surrounded by people. He had a rushing sound in his head and voices clamoured for his attention. A voice was asking him if he was hurt or had pain anywhere. He shook his head and murmured, 'the healer, please help the healer.'

Then more voices penetrated his head asking the crowd to move back, a man's face swam into view and Jacob muttered again, 'the healer, please help the healer.' The man moved his ear to Jacob's mouth. 'What's that son?' Jacob repeated the words and added, 'he is in the warehouse.' The paramedic was looking at him, 'have you been hurt son? You have blood all over you.'

Jacob shook his head, 'please please help him, he might die,'

The ambulance man looked at him and then spoke to his companion. 'Phone the police and get another crew here. It's all right son, we'll look after your friend. Now let's sort you out.' The man was examining his hands, which were covered in lacerations.

Another siren approached and a police car screamed to a halt. A burly police officer got out and asked him his name. He then spoke into his radio. 'Missing boy, Jacob Taylor has been found in Windsor St.'

The ambulance man said something to the officer who beckoned to his companion and they both ran off towards the warehouse. Relieved, Jacob allowed himself to be bundled into the back of the ambulance and they sped off towards the hospital. Then what occurred was a bewildering set of events. He was questioned by several police officers who were concerned about what the men had done to him in the warehouse. They seemed disinterested in the well being of the healer and disbelieving when Jacob told them about the ankle. 'Stockholm syndrome,' said one young woman to her companion. 'The boy has obviously got fond of his captor.'

'A bit quick for that, don't you think?' said the other officer.

Jacob was irritated by the exchange and told them so. He was even more irritated when his parents arrived and his mother burst into tears and sobbed all over him. Such a display of emotion had never happened before as far as Jacob could remember and he was intensely embarrassed. His dad stood to one side his arms hanging limply by his side and a goofy smile on his face. In a brief moment of respite, when his mother lifted her face to plant a kiss on his cheek, his dad stepped forward and patted him on his shoulder.

'Glad that you are safe, son,' he said. 'We are both going back to the family home for a few days. Mum and I are going to try and make a go of things again. Oh, and I have got a new job. So, things are looking up.' Jacob ducked under his mother's arm to avoid further unwelcome embraces. 'That's good,' he said simply. 'Can we get something to eat, I am starving.'

Much to Jacob's delight he was given a few days off from school to recover emotionally and physically. He could not hold a pen as his thumb and forefinger were badly cut but he was told he could use a computer to help him write. His dad bought him a new iPad to replace the one that had been taken although Jacob would have preferred it if his old one had been rescued. The school had tried to get it returned but the boys all denied taking it. Dad decided it would be quicker to sort out a new one while the school tried to get it back. Now that he was employed again his dad seemed to be filled with generosity.

On return to school he had been subjected to a long meeting with the Head of Year and his parents. He had had to give an undertaking to be polite and to stay in school. His parents had also had to sign a contract to say they would support the school in their attempts to support him. He was given an amber time out card that he could show to any teacher that allowed him to leave the room if he needed to. It all seemed a bit over the top, but he liked the fact that he had an excuse to get out of his least favourite lessons. At last, he was allowed back in form where he suddenly found he was a bit of celebrity. The other boys crowded around him wanting to know what had happened. He resisted the temptation to exaggerate his own role and enjoyed showing off his wounds. As he told his story for the hundredth time, he looked up and his eyes met those of the lad who had started the fight. He was standing in the doorway looking at him with such hatred in his eyes that Jacob had to turn away. A sense of foreboding hung over him. He had hoped things would improve but from the look on his face the lad had no intention of letting Jacob go.

Sure enough, that evening as Jacob walked home he heard footsteps running behind him. Someone pushed into him and pressed him against the wall. He could not see the face as it was hidden behind a scarf and a hood. The person said nothing but punched him in the gut. As Jacob doubled up he dropped the iPad to the floor. The figure stamped on it and then ran off. Jacob, gasping for breath felt tears springing into his eyes. Not again, he thought. Why me? Then a voice spoke to him asking him if he was all right. Jacob looked up at him. His face was vaguely familiar. As the man stooped to pick up the broken screen he realised it was the vicar who had conducted the christening.

'It's Jacob, isn't it? We met at the christening of David a few weeks ago. Let's go inside and take a few moments to get your breath back,' said the vicar. Jacob looked at him, tears streaming down his face; the shock of a second attack in a week was making him shake. The man took him by the elbow and led him to the church building opposite. Inside it was cool and dark. Jacob sat down on a chair near the door.

'So, do you want to tell me what happened?' asked the vicar. And despite himself, out it all came: the bullying, the fight, running away, the warehouse and now the attack. The vicar was a good listener; he didn't interrupt and revealed little through his expression. When Jacob finished the man looked at him. 'You have had a tough time Jacob. And you need to report this attack to your school. But do you know what happened to the man you called the healer?'

Jacob looked at his feet, 'No, but I did try and get him some help.' He looked again at the vicar and then lowered his eyes to the floor.

The vicar looked at him and then stood up. 'Come on, let's get you home.'

Rebekkah was at home when they got back. She was delighted to see the vicar again and made him a cup of tea. They sat and chatted about birds and books while Jacob phoned his dad and told him about the attack. Mr Taylor was furious and immediately contacted the school; they were of the view that the attack was nothing to do with them as it had happened outside school premises and as Jacob had not seen his attacker there was no reason to believe the suspect was a pupil at the school.

'They just don't care,' Jacob said to the vicar whose name was Steve.

'But you think it was the lad who has been taunting you?'

'Yes, but I can't prove it.'

Steve put his cup down very carefully on his saucer and looked at Jacob. 'Jacob, the world is full of injustice, and sometimes we get a chance to get our own back. However what goes around can come back to us. Consider carefully what you do before you act. Think about what sort of young man you wish to be.' And with that he left.

CHAPTER 17

JACOB

That night Jacob slept badly. His stomach was sore and his thoughts were troubled. He dreamt of eagles and magpies. They were battling together and it was bloody. The eagle had a nest and she was defending her young. The nest was under attack by hundreds of magpies. They wanted to kill and eat the little ones. The eagle was unable to defend herself because she needed to protect her young. Outnumbered she perched on the edge of her nest and spread out her enormous wings to cover her young. She lifted her proud head and cried, a loud yelping call that sounded more like a sea gull than a noble bird. He woke with a shout; his hands were bunched together and he was crying. He knew immediately what he must do.

The next morning, over breakfast he broached the subject that had been troubling him with his father. 'Dad, what happened to the man who helped me escape from the warehouse?'

His father looked up from his paper, 'The police arrested him along with that other criminal.'

'But that's not fair, he tried to help me. He shouldn't be treated the same as the magpie.'

'Why do you care? They are both losers.' His father looked at him. 'By the way, the police called, they want us to go back in to the station this morning. That bloke you call the healer has regained consciousness and has given a statement. They now want you to make another statement yourself.'

'Why? I told them what happened.' Jacob was impatient.

'They seem to think you were emotionally connected to the guy and now you have had a few days to think about it, they want you to give a clearer account of his involvement with your kidnapping.'

'He didn't kidnap me, I jumped into the warehouse and he tried to help me. It was that other guy, the magpie that tried to harm both of us. That's why the healer is so ill; the guy beat him to a pulp. I won't testify against him. Dad, you have got to help me. This is just not fair.' Jacob's face was pink, his chin jutted out in defiance and his eyes glistened. His father looked at him and slowly put down the paper. 'That guy really got to you, didn't he? Listen Jacob, there is something called Stockholm syndrome, which is where the people who have been kidnapped become emotionally attached to their kidnappers. We will need to get you some counselling if you aren't able to tell the truth.'

Jacob shouted and banged his fist on the table making the salt and pepper pots jump. 'I do not need counselling. I am not an emotional wreck; I just want to tell the truth and I want you to stick up for me and him.'

His dad looked at his watch. 'Let's go Jacob.'

Jacob looked at him and folded his arms. 'I am not going with you unless you promise to support my account.'

'How about you do as the police ask and then we can go and get you a new iPad? I don't want to spend all morning doing this.'

Jacob stood up, his fists were balls in his hands, anger like bile rose up in his throat. 'You think you can bribe me to lie? Just for an iPad, to say things that would put a man in jail. He is already down on his luck and now this. It's all because I tried to run away. I won't do it Dad and you will just have to sit with me until the police see sense!'

His dad looked at his watch and sighed. 'Okay. Now get in the car.'

Once they arrived at the station Mr Taylor asked to speak to the police officers in private. On returning to the interview room the officer was accompanied by a smart woman with a briefcase. They were then moved to a room that was more like a lounge and sat down together. The smart woman introduced herself as Dr Seymour and said she wanted to ask him a few more questions about the incident in the warehouse. Jacob looked at her and then at his father who shrugged.

'Are you a shrink?' he demanded.

'Jacob! Manners!' exclaimed his father.

'It's all right Mr Taylor. Yes, I am a psychiatrist and I would like you to give me your account of what happened. It's quite normal in these cases in order to help the victim come to terms with what has happened.'

Jacob looked at her with disdain. 'You won't change my story. I have already told the officers. I ran away from a fight at school. It was raining. I jumped into the warehouse to shelter and then I hurt my foot. The healer was there. He healed my foot with some ointment and then this other bloke arrived...'

'Ah yes,' interrupted the woman, 'healed your foot. Can we talk a bit more about that? What makes you so sure that your foot was badly hurt? Did he tell you it was?'

'No, it hurt. In fact I was in agony and I couldn't walk. I had to hop around.'

The lady turned to his father. 'Mr Taylor, has Jacob ever hurt his ankle before?'

Jacob's father looked at her. 'Not that I am aware of. Why?'

She was looking at the papers in front of her. 'Well the report from the doctor who attended Jacob in accident and emergency said that he x-rayed the foot and there definitely was a break, quite a nasty one, but it had healed. He said it was recent, within the last couple of months.'

Mr Taylor looked at his son. 'No, Jacob has never broken his ankle to my knowledge.' He shuffled awkwardly in his chair. 'Look is this necessary? Jacob may actually be telling the truth. Weird things do happen.'

The psychologist looked at him. 'It's understandable that you want to protect your son Mr Taylor but we do need him to testify to keep this dangerous child abductor off the streets. Otherwise he might do it again.'

'But Jacob was not abducted. He jumped into the warehouse. The guy happened to be there.'

'Ah but can we be sure? The behaviour of the man he calls magpie leads me to believe they were in this together. He abducted Jacob and pretended to be his friend. This is quite common in abductions, one kidnapper pretends to be the good cop and the other the bad cop.' She laughed, 'present company might recognise this technique in policing.' The officers smiled.

Jacob jumped up. 'This is ridiculous. You are twisting my words. He did not abduct me. I ran away from school because I was accused of starting a fight. The healer tried to help me. Why won't you listen?'

The lady rustled through her papers. 'It says on page four of your statement that the man you called the healer did not protect you from his companion and colluded with him when he phoned your father. Is that true?'

'Yes,' said Jacob through gritted teeth. 'But he obviously was planning how to help me because of what happened later. I don't know why he didn't help me earlier but have you considered that he might have had a plan and was waiting for a time when he could safely help me to leave?'

Dr Seymour was scribbling rapidly into a little red book. She looked up just once and smiled at Jacob and then went back to her writing. Then she stopped and fished out a photograph. 'Who is this Jacob?'

Jacob looked at the photo. It was the man he called the healer but his face was broken and bruised.

'The healer,' he whispered in a small voice.

She fished out another picture and gave to him. 'And who is this?'

Jacob expected to see the magpie in front of him. Instead he saw a different man, clean shaven and smiling. His arm was raised and perched on a leather sheath was a large golden eagle. His eyes however were unmistakably the same as those of the healer. 'I, I, I am not sure,' he stammered. 'I think it might be the healer.'

'You are right,' she gushed. 'This is Robert Seagull. Formerly, he worked as a bird-keeper at Beaulieu in Hampshire. He cared for the birds of prey there.'

'What happened to him?'

'Well, he was accused of stealing a golden eagle and selling it on the black market. He was sacked.' She paused.

Jacob opened his mouth to argue but she held up a hand to silence him. 'The eagle was later found. It had been poisoned, not as it happens by Robert, but by another bird-keeper who had been neglectful and left out meat with poison in it intended for rats. The eagle smelt the meat and ate it. The perpetrator, knowing he had been careless, allowed Robert to take the rap. So you see this is not the first time your friend has had a brush with the law.'

'So why are you telling me this? What has this got to do with my story?'

Dr Seymour paused and tapped her pen against her teeth. 'Let's just say that your friend Robert before he was sacked had been experimenting with healing ointments that he used to mend fractured wings on birds. So it may not be entirely inaccurate to say he helped your ankle.' The police officer seated to her right shifted slightly and stared at the doctor. 'Jacob, I find nothing in your story to lead me to believe that you are lying. In my expert opinion you have not got Stockholm syndrome and my recommendation is that your statement should be allowed to go forward as it is.'

The police officer stood up with Dr Seymour and the two of them walked out together. Shortly afterwards the officer returned alone. 'Just to let you know, based on your testimony Jacob, we are dropping charges against Robert Seagull but not against the man you call the magpie. However it may be of interest to you that when we entered the building Mr Seagull was on his own, the other man was nowhere to be seen and is still at large. So, without wishing to worry you, our advice is to be careful.'

Jacob shot up from his chair and whooped with joy.

CHAPTER 18

JACOB AND ROBERT SEAGULL

'Can I have some money Dad? I want to go into town, I am meeting John and some of my friends from school.' Absent-mindedly his dad placed some coins onto the table from his money purse and went back to watching the snooker.

It was Monday, two days after the interview in the police station. He took the number sixteen bus down to the hospital and walked into reception. He asked if they knew of the whereabouts of Robert Seagull. He was directed to the ward. Nervously, he entered the ward and was directed by the nurse at the desk to apply some disinfectant to his hands. Rubbing his hands together he marvelled at the way the slimy stuff just disappeared into his skin. As he passed through the ward he examined the occupants of the beds. Would he recognise the guy? Finally at the very end of the ward he saw him. His face was still swollen, his right eye puffy and black and one leg suspended in a cage above the bed. Jacob paused before walking purposefully on. He arrived at the bed and stood hesitantly to one side and waited. The man slowly turned his head and looked at him. He smiled revealing three cracked teeth.

'Hi Jacob,' he greeted him. 'It's good to see you again. Sit down, sorry I can't get up.'

Jacob looked for a chair and spied one at another bed. As he collected it he noticed the bedside cabinets of other people's beds were laden with fruit, sweets and soft drinks, Robert's was empty.

'I am sorry, I should have brought something for you,' he stammered.

Robert smiled, 'that's okay, you brought yourself; I wanted to thank you, for your testimony. The police have dropped all charges, I am free to go,' and he laughed, the deep laugh that Jacob remembered from the warehouse and waved vaguely at his leg. And then Jacob saw it. Robert was wearing a sleeveless vest and on his shoulder had been tattooed a beautiful golden eagle.

Robert followed Jacob's eyes and smiled. 'You are wondering about the eagle? She protects me.'

'Protects you!' Jacob blurted out. 'How can you believe that she protects you? You have lost everything; your job, your home, your... teeth! He looked at Robert who burst out laughing and stuck his tongue out through the gaps in his teeth.

'Yes, she protects me. Life often isn't fair and there are some really tough things along the way but you can either allow things to make you bitter or better. See, I am really lucky to have met you Jacob, because through your story Stephen your vicar friend came to see me. He has offered me food and accommodation if I look after the gardens at his church. So, all is well that ends well.'

Jacob looked at Robert, 'How did you know my name? And what do you know of the eagle?'

Robert looked back at him. 'Jacob all is not as it seems. Sometimes we have to trust and do what we believe is the right thing. Something tells me that you have not always been brave and honest; this is something you are learning. The eagle helps us to be strong and good and fair. Tell me? Did you call out to the eagle in the warehouse?'

Jacob looked at Robert. 'Maybe' he said after a long time. Robert smiled, his broken teeth gave him a weird lopsided appearance nonetheless the smile spread from his lips to his eyes and Jacob found himself looking into them and beyond. He thought he could see an eagle in her nest feeding her young but he could not be sure. He was reassured.

'She chose you Jacob, not the other way round. Your adventures are only just beginning. There is a deep magic at work in this world. It is where our world connects with the world of the nest. The eagle has her followers as you will discover.'

'Deep magic!' Jacob scoffed. 'I don't believe in...'

'...Magic.' Robert finished his sentence for him. 'Yes, I remember, you told me that in the warehouse. Well, it's not for me to persuade you.'

Jacob looked at him. 'Robert, there is something I have been wanting to ask you. Who is the magpie? He seemed to be your friend. Why didn't you warn me of him before he came back to the warehouse?'

Robert looked away and appeared to be thinking. A long time passed before he answered. 'Jacob, not everything can be explained in terms of flesh and blood and what we can see and feel. There are forces at work of good and evil. Sometimes it is not clear which one is which until much later. Even I can be deceived and I have been a follower of the eagle for many years. You have to be constantly on your guard. The magpie, as you call him, is clever. He appears in different forms but you will meet him again. Be on your guard. He is deceptive and catches us when we are weak. He can make us feel that he is our friend when really he plots our downfall.'

'Huh, that's not a very good explanation. He didn't catch me out. I knew he was evil right from the moment he opened the door.'

'Yes, that's when his true nature was revealed but up until then he was my friend. I thought him to be another homeless guy down on his luck just like me. He had helped me. It was only when you arrived that he changed and I realised who he was.'

'Mmm,' said Jacob sceptically. He looked carefully at the man he now called Robert. 'Why didn't you attack him straight away? Why did you go along with the phone call and frightening my dad? And why…' Jacob was growing more indignant as the memories flooded back, 'why did you tie me up? I had no chance of escaping.'

Robert looked at him sadly, all signs of merriment now drained from his face. 'Jacob, you have no idea of the forces of evil that follow the magpie. The only thing that works with him is to play him at his own game. Having revealed himself to you, my only strength was in knowing who he was. He however does not see the truth. I had a momentary advantage. I knew who he was but he didn't know who I was and so I played along with his game until a moment arrived to fight him. I slipped the glass to you so that you could escape. It was costly and I am sorry it had to be that way but you really don't know how strong he is. The outcome could have ended with your death.'

Ill-at-ease with all this talk of magic and forces, Jacob shuffled uneasily in his seat. It went against everything that he believed in. But he could not deny that he had dreamed about the eagle and her nest. Was it possible that another world existed and that somehow it was drawing him into it? He resolved to talk to Rebekkah when he left the hospital.

CHAPTER 19

REBEKKAH AND JACOB

Just as Jacob put his key into the door it flew open and his sister was standing, hands on hips, waiting for him. It was as if she knew that he wanted to talk to her.

'Where have you been?' she demanded. 'You can't just go off like that. The magpie is still around you know.'

He looked at her in astonishment. 'How did you know?' he asked her.

'Dad told me that we need to be careful because one of your abductors had run off, the one you called magpie.'

'Oh, that makes sense then. Bekkah, can we talk?'

He pushed past her and into the kitchen. She trotted after him expectantly. He was starving and began raiding the fridge and cupboards. He opened a packet of biscuits and shoved two into his mouth.

'Jacob that's really greedy,' Rebekkah reprimanded him. He hesitated planning to eat another two and then offered her the packet.

Shocked at this unusual act of brotherly kindness she took one and sat down with him at the table. He told her about the conversation with Robert at the hospital. She listened gravely. When he had finished she took another biscuit and then asked the question that had been on her lips since the journey to the nest.

'Jacob, what do you think happened at the nest?'

He looked at her turning a shade of pink at the memory. 'What do you remember?' he asked suspiciously.

She told him her account of what happened. Stunned at the accuracy of her memory he finally had to accept that they had both experienced something together in another world that transcended their own.

'So, what happens now?' he asked her.

Rebekkah shrugged. 'I guess we wait. It won't be long before the eagle contacts us again. And Robert seems to have warned you about the magpie. It sounds like he won't let you go.'

'We had better start looking out for each other then,' said Jacob gruffly.

'Fancy a strawberry milkshake?'